LIVING GOD'S WILL

Dwight L. Carlson, M.D.

Fleming H. Revell Company
Old Tappan, New Jersey

Library of Congress Cataloging in Publication Data

Carlson, Dwight L
   Living God's will.

   1. Christian life—1960-   2. God—Will.
I. Title.
BV4501.2.C315   248'.4   75-38860
ISBN 0-8007-0771-0 pbk.

TO Betty, with affection
my cherished best friend, companion, counselor,
sweetheart, and wife.

CONTENTS

PART THREE

SPECIFIC STEPS FOR KNOWING GOD'S WILL   105

PART FOUR

PREFACE

What is God's will for my life? That, it seems to me, is the most important question in life. Shortly after accepting Christ I attended a meeting where all who were willing to follow Christ, particularly in the form of missionary service, were encouraged to come forward. Wanting God's best for my life, I went forward. In fact, during those early years I raised my hand or went forward many dozens of times, indicating my willingness to fully yield my life to God. In the thirty years that have followed that initial decision, I have often reevaluated that primary question. How do I know God's will? What is His best for my life? Is God's best equated only with going to the mission field or some other form of full-time service?

Through the years I have heard many simplistic approaches to knowing God's will. One was the implication that anyone who wanted His best did, in fact, go to the mission field. Another, which seemed equally inadequate to me, was the principle illustrated by three harbor lights. This is the teaching that if God's Word, the Holy Spirit, and circumstances line up or agree, it must be God's will and so one should proceed. Is that really the whole truth regarding God's will for my life? In my pursuit to know God's will, I have read everything I could find on the subject and listened to every sermon available to me. I have prayerfully scrutinized the Scriptures to learn and apply the truths contained in them on this vital subject. This book, then, is the result of a lifelong pursuit to know God's will and live it. Included in the book are the principles on the subject that I feel are significant.

I am convinced that God wants every person to know and do His will, whether the person is ten or one hundred and ten, male or female, missionary or layman, street cleaner or professional. This book is *not* just for the college student who must decide on a career or the person trying to choose a life's mate. *It is not intended for the person seeking an easy way,* who wants to remain *superficial* or avoid getting involved with His Lord. Nor is it for the individual who is content with clichés and predictable or stock answers. *This is a book for the person who wants to make God the most important Person in his life,* more important than people, pleasures, money, or ego-gratification.

Just as there is no royal road to learning, there is no royal road to guidance. There are, however, some important principles which can help us discover and live God's will. I have listed these in as clear and precise a manner as I am able. I have included many scriptural references not only to verify the points being made but also so that the reader may study the principles involved (*see* Acts 17:11).

Many of the principles discussed on these pages won't be assimilated into one's life by reading about them once or even several times. Therefore, questions have been added to the end of each chapter not only for individual consideration but preferably for group discussion as well. Others desirous of knowing and living God's will can be of immense help to you—and you to them —in understanding and applying His will. The questions marked with an asterisk (*) should probably be answered anonymously. This can be achieved by passing out paper and pencil to each person in your study group. Have each person write his answer without signing his name. Then collect, mix, and redistribute. The answers can then be shared and discussed.

I want to express my appreciation to Mrs. Pam Hansman for typing the manuscript several times. Helpful suggestions were made by H. Norman Wright, Reverend Randolf Klassen, Reverend Gary Copeland, Dr. Norman Harris, and Miss Carla Stayboldt. I also want to thank Mrs. Marilyn McGinnis for her helpful editing.

Greatly appreciated is the support and understanding of our two wonderful children, Susan and Gregory. Last, but certainly not least, I want to express gratitude to my dear wife, Betty, for her valuable help with this book and for her continued encouragement as we endeavor together to live in His perfect will.

DWIGHT L. CARLSON

LIVING GOD'S WILL

PART ONE
THE NATURE OF GOD'S WILL

God *"has made known* to us in all wisdom and insight *the mystery of his will . . ."* (Ephesians 1:9 author's italics). Paul's earnest desire and prayer for the New Testament believers was ". . . that you may be *filled with the knowledge of his will* in all spiritual wisdom and understanding, *to lead a life worthy of the Lord,* fully pleasing to him, bearing fruit in every good work and increasing in the knowledge of God" (Colossians 1:9, 10 author's italics).

I believe there are many sincere Christians who frequently "stub their toes" in the Christian life because they simply don't understand the nature or characteristics of God's will. The first part of this book is directed at helping you better understand God's will so that you may be able to live it.

1
YOU CAN BE IN HIS PERFECT WILL

On New Year's Day, 1929, Georgia Tech played the University of California in the Rose Bowl. In that game a man named Roy Riegels recovered a fumble for California. Somehow, he became mixed up and started running in the wrong direction. One of his team mates outdistanced him and downed him just before he scored for the opposing team. Tech took the ball on down and scored and that touchdown was the margin of victory.

That strange play came in the first half, and everyone who was watching the game was asking the same question: "What will Coach Nibbs Price do with Roy Riegels in the second half?" The men filed off the field and went into the dressing room. They sat down on the benches and on the floor, all but Riegels. He put his blanket around his shoulders, sat down in a corner, put his face in his hands, and cried like a baby.

If you have played football, you know that a coach usually has a great deal to say to his team during half time. That day Coach Price was quiet. No doubt he was trying to decide what to do with Riegels. Then the time keeper came in and announced that there were three minutes before playing time. Coach Price looked at the team and said simply, "Men, the same team that played the first half will start the second."

The players got up and started out, all but Riegels. He did not budge. The coach looked back and called to him again; still he didn't move. Coach Price went over to where Riegels sat and said, "Roy, didn't you hear me? The same team that played the first half will start the second." Then Roy Riegels looked up and his cheeks were wet with a strong man's tears. "Coach," he said, "I can't do it to save my life. I've ruined you, I've ruined the University of California, I've ruined myself. I couldn't face that crowd in the stadium to save my life." Then Coach Price reached out and put his hands on Riegels' shoulder and said to him: "Roy, get up and go on back; the game is only half over." And Roy Riegels went back, and those Tech men will tell you that they have never seen a man play football as Roy Riegels played that second half.

When I read that story, deep inside I said, "What a coach!" When I read the story of Jonah and the story of a thousand lives like his, I say, "What a God!" We take the ball and run in the wrong direction; we stumble and fall and are so ashamed of ourselves that we never want to try again, and He comes to us and bends over us in the person of His Son and says, "Get up and go on back; the game is only half over." That is the gospel of the grace of God. It is the gospel of a second chance, of a third chance, of the hundredth chance.

HADDON W. ROBINSON, Ph.D.
From *Focal Point*, publication of the Christian Medical Society.

Jonah learned this startling truth despite the fact that he had deliberately and consciously disobeyed God. Nevertheless, "The word of the LORD came to Jonah *the second time . . .*" (Jonah 3:1 author's italics). God's long-suffering allows us over and over again to start anew. It's easy for us to forget this and Satan takes advantage of the situation if he can. In fact, one of his big lies is to get us to think that because we have "blown it" in the past (which we all have), it is impossible for us to be in the center of God's perfect will. After all, he argues, that past sin or wrong decision will surely keep you from God's best. So you have to be content with God's second, or third, or fourth best. Oh, you'll get to heaven alright, but don't expect a fulfilled, purposeful life. This kind of reasoning keeps many people out of God's perfect will. Satan does this by having us think that God's will is like a straight road between two points with just enough gas in the tank to reach the ultimate goal. This is illustrated below.

Satan's lie about God's will

Starting   Ultimate
Point   Goal

With this understanding about God's will it is obvious that any wrong move will prevent you from ever reaching the ultimate point; therefore, you will miss the mark—God's perfect will. This misconception is illustrated below.

God's will impossible to reach

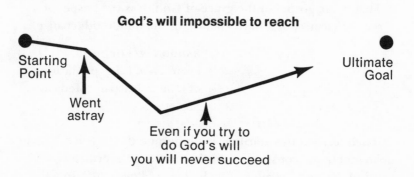

Starting   Ultimate
Point   Goal

Went
astray

Even if you try to
do God's will
you will never succeed

It is true that none of us will ever live up to God's initial intended perfect will throughout our life. We have all sinned and thus have missed the mark. However, Psalms 130:3, 4 reminds us of how great a God we have: "If thou, O LORD, shouldst mark iniquities, Lord, who could stand? But there is forgiveness with thee. . . ." God's will can be properly viewed as a target with His perfect will the bull's-eye. The choice is up to us if we want to aim for God's perfect will at any moment in time. Unconfessed past sin must be cleared by admitting our sin and accepting God's forgiveness. Then our efforts must be directed to the present. God's concern and orientation is for the now. It also includes our intentions for the future, but the main force of our energy must be directed to the present. *The highest will of God is that now—wherever I find myself—I am doing what pleases Him the most.*

I may have some scars from being out of God's will in the past, but despite the scars He wants to make me into a beautiful person. Satan would just love to have me think that because of the scars (depicting sin or time lost in the past) I am utterly useless for the rest of my life. I am a second-rate citizen and bound to be unhappy and unsuccessful. This attitude is dead wrong. It is true that scars leave their permanent effects. Yet God's recreative powers are tremendous. He may not erase every last scar, but He will make me into an attractive person who will be satisfying to me and Him.

Let's look further in the Scriptures for some examples of those whom God used after they "blew it." Abraham used deceit in Genesis 20, yet he was esteemed one of the highest patriots of old. Moses was a murderer, yet was chosen by God to be the great leader of Israel. Rahab was a prostitute and a liar. Yet she was physically saved and praised in the Hall of Faith in Hebrews 11 without mention of her years of debauchery. King David won favor in God's eyes and yet committed more infamous acts than some of our recent leaders. He not only committed adultery but also murder. Yes, some scars were left as a result of this, but he still is mentioned as a man after God's own heart (*see* Acts 13:22).

It amazes me to see again God's recreative and forgiving capabilities. In the genealogy of Christ we find that both Rahab the harlot and Bathsheba the beautiful woman taken in adultery were involved in Christ's ancestry. Here God uses these sin-touched lives in His most beautiful redemptive act—Christ. And of course the disciples "blew it" many times. Peter, the man on whom Christ would build His church, adamantly denied Him three times. John Mark was a quitter whom God was willing to use after the most prominent Christian leader of the day had rejected him.

When you are tempted to think that because you have sinned, because you have wasted years, because you have taken a major erroneous road, you can't be in God's perfect will—don't you believe it. God has promised us in His Word that He will pass our sins behind His back, never to be remembered again (*see* Isaiah 38:17; 43:25). No matter what sin you have committed in the past, if you are only willing, God will take you now where you are and make you into a beautiful instrument that will glorify Him. Even if another person has hurt you or has sinned in such a way that it has affected or is affecting your life, God will take what was possibly meant for ill and make something beautiful out of it even as He did with Joseph (*see* Genesis 50:20). This means that *no other person or situation can keep you from God's perfect will for your life.* That is, no other person except yourself. If you are married, for example, and your spouse is not a Christian, or is a very carnal Christian, he or she cannot keep you from being in God's perfect will.

Look at 1 Samuel 8 for an illustration of the same act being in God's permissive will for one person and God's perfect will for another. Israel wanted a king. God didn't want them to have a king. Samuel was sensitive to God's perfect will and likewise did not want a king. But the people pressed the issue, so God let them have their way. God told Samuel to anoint the king, an act which was within God's perfect will for Samuel, but only in His permissive will for the Israelites. And as almost inevitably is the case in God's permissive will, subsequent years were filled with misery for the nation of Israel. (Chapter 5, "There Are Degrees of His Will," covers in depth God's perfect and permissive will.)

One last comment to those who are older in years. Satan uses the same reasoning to try to dissuade you from really yielding your all to God at this late stage in life. You question, "What's the use now? I've wasted most of my life." This kind of reasoning is not of God. He wants you to consider the now, and to be obedient in the now. I am sure it is difficult for somebody who is fifty, sixty, or seventy years of age to start afresh in yielding his life completely to God. However, be encouraged, for Matthew 20 tells us that those who only labor a very short time in the Lord's kingdom may be rewarded equally with those who have yielded their life from a very early age.

One brief word of warning to anyone who might use this chapter as an excuse to continue in sin and then "someday" get right with God. God's Word clearly warns that "My spirit shall not always strive with man" (Genesis 6:3 KJV). A person who continues to sin willfully may actually have no interest later in spiritual things or in doing God's will because God's Spirit is no longer drawing him (*see* John 6:44).

But to any person reading these pages who has even a slight interest in God's will—to you, I believe, God is now making available His perfect will for your life—if you want it. Such a person must be willing to forget the past and actively seek to live His will now and in the future (*see* Philippians 3:13, 14).

QUESTIONS FOR INDIVIDUAL AND GROUP CONSIDERATION

1. Do you really believe any person can be in God's perfect will? Do you believe you can be in God's perfect will?

2. Is there any person, circumstance, or thing that can keep you from God's perfect will?

3. Jack and Rosemary were married several years ago. Since then Rosemary became acquainted with a group of Christian women

in her neighborhood and was ultimately led to a personal relationship with Christ. She is now eager to be in God's perfect will. She is studying her Bible and wants to continue to attend a women's Bible study. She also wants to attend Sunday school and church and take her children with her. She would love to have her husband come also but he not only refuses to attend, he is also adamantly against her having anything to do with religion. What should she do? Can she be in God's perfect will?

4. Why do people often use wrong decisions and past sin as an *excuse* to keep from doing God's will now? Do some people really think they cannot now be in His perfect will? Does one's ego ever get involved? How?

5. Do you think God really forgets our past sin just as if it never occurred? Do we really believe this? What are the ramifications?

6. Mr. and Mrs. Jones are sixty years of age. They accepted Christ many years ago and have attended church faithfully. They are "good people" but have never wanted to be, as they put it, "fanatics." They have maintained the right over their own lives. Now they realize that they have been carnal Christians, living at best within God's permissive will. They are not aware of any unusual natural talents or abilities. Can Mr. and Mrs. Jones now be in God's perfect will, leading full, meaningful, productive Christian lives? How would they go about doing this? What changes would you anticipate? Is it possible that God might reward them as much for a few years of yielded service in their 60s as He would a young couple who have been yielded throughout all of their adult life? Is this fair?

2

LIVING GOD'S WILL IS THE GREATEST THING THAT CAN HAPPEN TO YOU

Living God's will is the greatest thing that can ever happen to you. Stop reading for a moment and let that magnificent thought sink in. Romans 12:2 states, *". . . the plan of God for you is good . . ."* (PHILLIPS). Repeatedly in the Scriptures we find God wanting great things for His people—but unfortunately, they often resist His will and thus His blessing. Christ wept over the people in Jerusalem because they were unwilling to accept His love and will. The Israelites were told, ". . . what does the Lord your God require of you except to listen carefully to all he says to you, and to obey *for your own good . . ."* (Deuteronomy 10:12, 13 LB author's italics).

Romans 12:2 further states, ". . . that the *plan of God for you is good,* meets all His demands and moves toward the goal of true maturity" (PHILLIPS, author's italics). John 10:10 tells us, "I came that they may *have life,* and have it *abundantly"* (author's italics). And Romans 8:28 states, "Moreover we know that to those who love God, who are called according to his plan, everything that happens fits into a *pattern for good"* (PHILLIPS, author's italics).

Often people around us make demands upon us that are overwhelming. Sometimes these demands come from well-meaning religious people. But God's demands are never more than we can bear. In fact 1 John 5:3 states, "Loving God means doing what he tells us to do, and really, that isn't hard at all" (LB). Other translations say, "And his commandments are not burdensome" (RSV) or "grievous" (KJV). Deuteronomy 30:11 reassures us, "Obeying these commandments is not something beyond your strength and reach" (LB).

I am well aware of the verses that state, "I die every day" (1
Corinthians 15:31) and, "If any man would come after me, let
him deny himself and take up his cross daily and follow me"
(Luke 9:23). Certainly obedience necessitates discipline and a
willingness to undergo hardship. However, I believe that in the
free world much of the difficulty that Christians face is not necessary and is not of God. Sin, partial obedience, pressure from
men, or even well-meaning Christian leaders, so often extract a
tremendous toll from our lives. Medically, at least 50 percent of
illness and suffering is self-induced. Unfortunately, many who
bear the name of Christ fall into this same category. Satan's big
lie is to have us think that God's plan and will for us is far more
difficult than it actually is or that for some reason we can't realize
His great will for our lives. If he can achieve this, he can discour-
age us from ever taking up our cross and following Christ. He
also blinds people to the fact that they are already carrying a
heavy burden which Christ wants to remove and replace with a
much lighter one (*see* Matthew 11:28–30).

Furthermore, from the eternal perspective God's plan is un-
deniably good. When we consider that life is just for a moment
in comparison to eternity which is forever, it totally upsets the
balance of what a good life is. It's so difficult for us time-bound
creatures to see things from the eternal perspective. Maybe an
illustration can help. Imagine a line extended from the left side
of this page to the right side, then off the page indefinitely. One
thirty-second of an inch on the left side may well represent your
life here on earth while the remainder of the unending line repre-
sents eternity. This helps give a little better perspective of time
and eternity. God has promised that He will forever wipe away
all tears and suffering and that in His eternal presence will be
fullness of joy and pleasures forevermore (*see* Revelation 21:1–4;
Psalms 16:11).

"I will instruct you (says the Lord) and guide you along the best
pathway for your life; I will advise you and watch your progress"
(Psalms 32:8 LB).

When God instructed Moses to lead the children of Israel into the Promised Land, Moses needed further assurance. " 'please, if this is really so, guide me clearly along the way you want me to travel so that I will understand you and walk acceptably. . . .' And the Lord replied, 'I myself will go with you and give you success' " (Exodus 33:13, 14 LB).

QUESTIONS

*1. If you could ask God one question, what would it be?

2. Do you really believe at the deep, inner level that God's complete will for your life is the greatest thing that could happen to you? Do you think of God as a killjoy who would squelch your life if you gave Him the chance?

3. Is His will for our life really good, or is that a come-on? Is it true for the missionary? for a person in a country where Christians are persecuted?

4. Do you agree that a lot of the problems and sufferings we Christians have are of our own making? Give a firsthand example.

5. What was the joy set before Christ that helped Him endure the cross? (*See* Hebrews 12:2.) In what way might this be applied to us?

6. Which fear do you think is more common among Christians:
    (a) fear of what might happen if out of the will of God
    (b) fear of where obedience might lead (God will make a fool out of you; He will take away all meaningful life, etc.). Which do you fear?

7. Recently I read this statement, "Success is inevitable when you stand in the place that pleases God." Is this true? All kinds of success? The book continues, "You have been redeemed from every sickness, you have been redeemed from fear, you have been redeemed from poverty." Are all of these guaranteed to every obedient Christian?

3

GOD WANTS TO REVEAL HIS WILL TO YOU

God has promised He will reveal His will to us. Psalms 32:8 states,
"I will instruct thee and teach thee in the way which thou shalt go:
I will guide thee with mine eye" (KJV author's italics). Isaiah 30:21
tells us, "And your ears shall hear a word behind you, saying,
'This is the way, walk in it, when you turn to the right or when
you turn to the left.' " And Proverbs 3:5, 6 says, "Trust in the
Lord with all thine heart; and lean not unto thine own understanding. In all thy ways acknowledge him, and *he shall direct thy
paths"* (KJV author's italics).

We are not only promised that God will reveal His will to us;
He also commands us to know His will. Ephesians 5:17 states, "Therefore do not be foolish, but understand what the will of the Lord
is." And Romans 12:2 says, "Do not be conformed [a command]
to this world but be transformed [a command again] by the
renewal of your mind, [how] that you may [means] prove what is
the will of God, what is good and acceptable and perfect."

Not only has He promised to reveal His will to us and commanded that we know it but He also promises that *it is available
to us.* Deuteronomy 30:14 says, "But the word is very near you;
it is in your mouth and in your heart, so that you can do it." Isaiah
58:11 promises, "The LORD will guide you continually."

Although God wants to reveal His will to us *He will not force it
upon us.* We must carefully listen or we will, in fact, miss it. Look
again at Psalms 32:8, 9, which says, "I will instruct thee and teach
thee in the way which thou shalt go: I will guide thee with mine
eye. Be ye not as the horse, or as the mule, which have no
understanding: whose mouth must be held in with bit and bridle,
lest they come near unto thee" (KJV). These verses indicate that

the Lord will instruct, lead, and teach us His will for our lives. This includes His general overall plan as well as the specifics. Many times I have pondered the meaning of "I will guide thee with mine eye." Have you ever watched a person direct his or her spouse or child to do something in a large room full of people —without saying a word or moving a hand? Just the slight movement of the eyes, detected only by the attentive individual, clearly conveys the command. So God may direct us from one course to another as quietly but decisively as the mere movement of His eyes. Such direction requires that we are carefully looking to God for direction. Otherwise we will miss His direction. Psalms 32:9 goes on to say that *He will not* lead us as a mule or as a horse which has no understanding and which must be forcefully manipulated.

"The Lord will guide you continually, and satisfy you with all good things . . ." (Isaiah 58:11 LB).

QUESTIONS

1. Why do you want to know God's will for your life? List all the reasons.

2. Do you ever feel you have done everything you should and God hasn't done His part by revealing His will to you? If God hasn't revealed His will to you, what are the possible reasons?

3. Is the promise that He will reveal His will for every person? If there are any exceptions, who are they?

4. Romans 8:14 says, "For all who are led by the Spirit of God are sons of God." Does this mean every Christian is led? Does this mean anyone not led by God is not a Christian?

4

MOST OF HIS WILL FOR YOU IS ALREADY REVEALED

"The whole Bible was given to us by inspiration from God and is useful to teach us what is true and to make us realize what is wrong in our lives; it straightens us out and it helps us do what is right. It is God's way of making us well prepared at every point, fully equipped to do good to everyone" (2 Timothy 3:16, 17 LB).

The entire purpose of God's Word is to teach us His truths and show us how to live this life. Some of the last verses in the Bible warn us that His basic revelation for man is complete (*see* Revelation 22:18, 19). This, of course, does not mean that we aren't led by the Holy Spirit in the day-by-day aspects of our life but it certainly does mean that the basic important truths have already been clearly revealed to us.

Deuteronomy 30:11–20 says in part that His will is "not too hard . . . neither is it far off." It further says that His Word "is very near you . . . so that you can do it." Isaiah 28:13 speaks about His Word being ". . . precept upon precept, precept upon precept line upon line, line upon line, here a little, there a little. . . ." The Living Bible puts it this way: "The Lord will spell it out for them again, repeating it over and over in simple words whenever He can. . . ." So we find that those things which are most important to God's will are repeatedly revealed to us in His Word.

God has gone to great efforts to clearly reveal His will to us, even to give it to us in written form. So often we are unwilling to take the time to really know what the Bible has already told us to do. We may even be too busy with "God's work." Instead we run around seeking God's will from other sources. More will be said about the important place of God's Word in seeking and doing His will in chapter 24.

Personally, I have my hands full being obedient to the things God has already revealed to me. If God were to say to me, "Dwight, I am not going to reveal one more aspect to you regarding My will. I have given you My Word; dig into it, find out what I have been saying to men down through the ages, and to the best of your ability follow it"—I would have my hands full just completing that. He has already told us He wants us to set out to do His revealed will first. As we do it we should always remain open to further direction from Him regarding the details. If He reveals any special instructions to us we must follow them. Otherwise, we continue the course He has already laid down in the Scriptures.

I often liken this to the way big business sets up a branch office (*see* Matthew 24:45, 46; 25:14–29). Let's say a large company based in Chicago sends me to the Los Angeles area to represent them. My job is to open an office and sell a given product which they are manufacturing. After a conference with the president of the company, I set out for Los Angeles. As a trusted executive my job is to fulfill the wishes of the president of the company, and I pretty well know what they are.

Now I could call the president ten times a day with numerous questions. Should I go out to lunch with Mr. Jones? Should I paint the inside of the office a light brown or white? Do you think I should hire Jane or Brenda as secretary? After a few such calls the president would probably say, "Hey, Dwight, use your brain. You've got one, you know what we want, you've interviewed the people. Use your best judgment and get on with the job." On the other hand, if some more important issue comes up certainly a phone call is in order. Weekly or monthly reports are essential and if the president calls me and says he knows an excellent secretary just leaving the Chicago area whom I should hire, these instructions should be carefully followed.

I am not saying God put us on the earth and turned His back on us; or that He is not interested in the minutiae of our lives. Nor am I saying that we should not daily seek His will for our lives. The point I am trying to make is that *He has revealed* the basics of His will and really expects us to follow through on these using good judgment. When Paul was going to preach, he set out to do the job which he knew was on Christ's heart. Acts 15:36 tells us, "And after some days Paul said to Barnabas, 'Come, let us return and visit the bretheren in every city where we proclaimed the word of the Lord, and see how they are.' " There doesn't appear to be any supernatural call for this particular missionary journey. The people were on his heart and Paul knew that it was Christ's will to nourish these new Christians. As Paul set about to do this work he was forbidden by the Holy Spirit to preach in Asia (*see* Acts 16). So they went to Bithynia, but again the Spirit prohibited their preaching in that area. Later the Holy Spirit directed them to Macedonia. Thus Paul was doing the logical thing in fulfilling Christ's great concern, and *while moving* on this missionary journey, he was directed.

It is kind of like a ship. You can only change its course if it is moving. *Many times we don't know God's will because we are not moving —doing those things already clearly revealed in the Scriptures.* Abraham's servant is another beautiful example of this principle (*see* Genesis 24). He set out with some basic instructions in mind, stating, "I being in the way, the Lord led me . . ." (verse 27 KJV). *As he set out to do God's will, God then specifically directed him.*

Thus I believe most of His will for you and me is already revealed. All we need to do is look into the Scriptures for it. It takes more than a casual look, however. We must study the Word —saturation combined with obedience. Then as we are moving along only a slight tug at the wheel by the Master will direct our course differently if that is His will for us (*see* Isaiah 30:21).

QUESTIONS

1.   Joe is a freshman in college. He is currently spending many hours trying to make the following decisions:
     (a) what his major should be
     (b) what occupation he should pursue

(c) whether he should go into full-time Christian service

(d) whom to marry

The specifics of these questions are not answered in the Bible. From Joe's perspective most of God's will for him is *not* already revealed. How does this chapter relate to his specific situation?

2. To what extent is the illustration of a corporation in Chicago sending an executive to Los Angeles an appropriate parallel to our relationship with God? In what way does the illustration fall short?

3. Could you live a life pleasing to God if the only means of guidance for you was the Bible?

5
THERE ARE DEGREES OF HIS WILL

There are various degrees of God's will. At least three can be clearly seen in the Scriptures. A person or a particular activity can be in God's *perfect will,* in His *permissive will,* or totally *out of His will.*

The non-Christian remains *out of God's will.* Romans 3:23 states, "All have sinned and fall short of the glory of God." Left to our own devices we all totally miss the mark. "The wages of sin is death . . ." (Romans 6:23). Eternal separation from God is the consequence of being out of God's will. Isaiah 64:6 says, "We have all become like one who is unclean, and all our righteous deeds are like a polluted garment. We all fade like a leaf, and our iniquities, like the wind, take us away." In other words, even noteworthy deeds that an individual might do will not rectify the situation if the person has missed the mark before God's eyes by not accepting Christ's Provision.

Unfortunately, even the "Christian" may be grossly out of God's will. At one time he accepted Christ but now in at least one area of his life he has "done his own thing." In 1 John 1:8 we read, "If we say we have no sin, we deceive ourselves, and the truth is not in us." Fortunately it does not stop there, for the ninth verse says, "If we confess our sins, he is faithful and just, and will forgive our sins and cleanse us from all unrighteousness." John beautifully sums up why the Scriptures were given in 1 John 2:i when he says, "My little children, I am writing this to you so that you may not sin; but if any one does sin, we have an advocate with the Father, Jesus Christ the righteous."

I believe one can be living in God's *permissive will.* This is a state where one has allowed certain thoughts or activities that fail to meet His perfect or ideal aspiration for one's life. There may not always be overt sin involved.

Degrees of God's Will

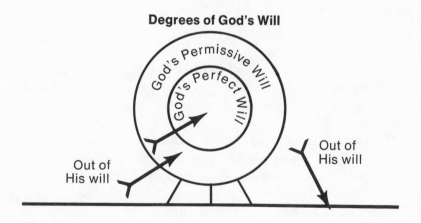

Let's look into the Bible for some examples. In Mark 10:2–9 it says that God allowed divorce though it was not His original intent. Hebrews 12:1 tells us not only to lay aside any sin, but also "every weight" (KJV). Things in our life which are not sin but weights place us in God's permissive will. Balaam in Numbers 22 is an excellent example of a man who wanted the best of two worlds and got the worst of both. You will recall that Balak wanted Balaam to go and curse God's people, the Israelites. Balaam told Balak to wait overnight and he would pray about the matter. God's reply to Balaam was that he should not go, which Balaam told the messengers of Balak. However, Balak was not satisfied, so the messengers returned to Balaam and pressed him further. He asked God a second time and God's reply was, "Rise, go with them" (verse 20). Though this was from God it was clearly His permissive will. Balaam went, but in the process incurred God's anger and faced all kinds of trouble. He lost face with Balak and eventually was killed with the heathen. He tried to please himself and other men and instead obtained the wrath of both God and man.

Another vivid example is that of the Israelites. Psalms 106:12–15 says, "Then believed they his words; they sang his praise. They soon forgat his works; they waited not for his counsel: But lusted exceedingly in the wilderness, and tempted God in the desert. And he gave them their request; but sent leanness into their soul" (KJV). Here God gave the Israelites their request, His permissive will, but with it came the conseqences of His permissive will, internal void.

A classic example of God's permissive will was when the Israelites appointed a king. This was clearly not His ideal or perfect will. But at the repeated insistence of the people, God yielded. When the king was anointed by the command of God, He made it very clear who was responsible—the people. As is typical with His permissive will, there was an added responsibility and warning. The Israelites were admonished not only to listen, love, and serve the Lord but also that *both* the people and the king were responsible for a favorable result (*see* Deuteronomy 17:14–20; Judges 8:22–24; 1 Samuel 8:14–18; 12:12–24).

A fourth example of God's permissive will is the righteous King Hezekiah's crying to God to extend his life (*see* 2 Kings 20; 2 Chronicles 32; Isaiah 38). He had been faithful to God up to this point, but during an additional fifteen years granted through God's permissive will he became proud and disobedient. His sons likewise were sinful and ended up as slaves. These were the end results of seeking God's permissive will. Hezekiah would have been better off dying earlier but remaining in God's perfect will.

It is of significance that in almost every instance where God's permissive will was deliberately sought the results turned out badly. A person who is satisfied with God's *permissive will* usually ends up *out of His will* (*see* 1 Kings 12:30; 13:34). As I muse on my own life there are many things that I have done out of God's will and a few things that may or may not have been out of His will or in His permissive will. (I am not wasting any time trying to figure out which category they were in—they have been dealt with and I am going on.) However, at least two activities which I became involved with were—it seems to me—in God's permissive will. One was buying a new car for which I had to overextend myself, and the other was dating a girl who by her own admission was not deeply interested in a spiritual life. I really was not happy until I eventually sold the car and broke off the relationship with the girl.

Now let's turn our attention to God's *perfect will.* The story of Mary and Martha in Luke 10:40–42 tells of two individuals who deeply loved Christ. Martha was very busy preparing a meal, possibly for Christ; Mary, on the other hand, was sitting at His feet listening to Him teach. Martha was upset over doing the work alone and asked Christ to intervene, to which He responded, "Only a few things are really needed, perhaps only one. Mary has chosen the *best* part and you must not tear it away from her!" (Luke 10:42 PHILLIPS, italics author's). In Philippians 1:9, 10 Paul says, "And it is my prayer that your love may abound more and more, with knowledge and all discernment, so that you may approve what is excellent. . . ." As previously mentioned, Acts 13:22 tells us that David was a man after God's own heart. He really hit the bull's-eye. And who typifies remaining always in God's perfect will more than Christ? In John 8:29 He says, "I always do what is pleasing to him."

Obviously God's perfect will is what we should be always striving for in our lives. Jude admonishes, "Stay always within the boundaries where God's love can reach and bless you" (Jude verse 21 LB). The Psalmist says, "Where is the man who fears the Lord? God will teach him how to choose the best. He shall live within God's circle of blessing . . ." (Psalms 25:12, 13 LB).

QUESTIONS

1. Do you agree that there are various degrees in God's will? Some Bible scholars believe one is either in God's perfect will or out of His will. What do you think? Why?

*2. What percentage of the time do you live (a) in God's perfect will, (b) in God's permissive will, (c) outside God's will?

3. Can the same activity or thing change categories? For example, can something be in God's perfect will at one time, later be in His permissive will, and subsequently be out of His will? Can you give a scriptural or personal example?

4. Is there anyone who cannot be in God's perfect will? What if a person married outside of His will? is divorced? is a murderer?

*5. As we look at the individuals around Christ we find four groups: (1) the multitudes who were basically onlookers, (2) the seventy disciples who followed Him for a while but when things got a little tough they deserted Him, (3) the twelve apostles who left everything and followed Christ, (4) the three apostles who were closest to Christ and who loved Him the most. In which group would you place yourself? Do you want to be in a group closer to Christ? Do you really want to live in His perfect will? Is one's position static?

6. Is it always wrong to ask the Lord the second time for instructions? *See* 1 Samuel 23:1–4. What makes the difference?

7. Three Christian couples are in the market to buy a home. It turns out that each of them buys a home for seventy-five thousand dollars. Is it possible that one couple is in God's perfect will, the second couple is in His permissive will, and the third couple is out of His will? Explain. Is this fair?

6
GOD'S WILL IS PERSONAL

There are many aspects of God's will that are applicable and identical for everyone. It is God's will that none perish, but that all should have eternal life (*see* Matthew 18:14; 1 Timothy 2:4; 2 Peter 3:9). It is His will that all should forsake sin and worship Him. It is His will that all should be nourished in God's Word and grow to maturity. Whether you are a minister, missionary, businessman, or housewife, He expects you to live a holy life.

Yes, it's true that many aspects are applicable for all. However, some people would like to go beyond the basics and put us all into the same mold. By failing to realize that the personal leading of God is different for every person, they subtly manipulate or pressure others to conform to their idea of God's will. For example, some well-meaning Christians suggest that *every* really yielded Christian should be on the mission field or in full-time Christian work. This has a devastating effect on the immature Christian who is struggling to know God's will. "Among Christians," says Elisabeth Elliot in her provocative and delightful book *A Slow and Certain Light,* "it is pestilently evil to make the exceptional experience of some the rule of faith for all." Some will make a spiritual experience a status symbol and get the person's eyes off of Christ and on to things. Oswald Chambers has said, "Don't make a principle out of your experience, let God be as original with others as He was with you." Although many aspects of God's will are applicable to all, many are very, very personal and individual.

Peter, wondering about John's relationship to Christ, "asked Jesus, 'What about him, Lord?' . . . Jesus replied . . . 'what is that to you? *You* follow me' " (John 21:21, 22 LB). Christ told one man to go home, another to follow Him, one to be silent, and another to witness (*see* Matthew 10:5–7; Mark 5:14–19; Luke 5:27; 9:23). Stephen, a faithful follower of Christ, was the first martyr and died at an early age. John the Apostle, who followed Christ for a long period of time, died a natural death at a ripe old age. Paul was in prison for years, yet God chose to miraculously deliver Peter the very first night of his imprisonment. John 10:3–9 reminds us that He calls us by name, indicating a very personal relationship and will for our lives.

Some people are rich, some are poor, some are healed, others are allowed to bear their "thorn in the flesh" (2 Corinthians 12:7 KJV). Some emphatically believed that it was within God's will, for instance, to lie to Hitler's troupers in order to save the lives of Jewish people in hiding. Others, just as sincere and devoted to Christ, were not able to do that within God's will. Even in our day there are some great Christians who believe it is God's will to use questionable methods to get God's Word behind the Iron Curtain; others believe it is wrong. Paul's exhortation that we not criticize another for having different ideas from ours about what is right and wrong certainly applies. He goes on to say that on certain aspects of God's will "every one must decide for himself" (LB), or as the Revised Sandard translation puts it, "Let every one be fully convinced in his own mind" (Romans 14:5).

So when you consider God's will for your life—or for others—

remember God knows you as a person and may lead you in a way which is slightly different from every other human being (*see* Exodus 33:12–17; John 21:15–22).

QUESTIONS

1. Do you believe and *feel* at a deep, inner level that God personally knows you apart from every other human being on the earth? Does God *really love you*? Does he *really care* about your well-being?

2. Does God really have a personal will for you that is different from any other human being? What is the danger of pushing this idea too far?

3. Do you ever feel that others think they know God's will for you in areas where they frankly don't? Give an example. How do you handle such situations?

4. Have you ever been guilty of thinking you know God's will for another person (apart from the general areas of His desire that all individuals be reconciled to Him)? What is the most recent example?

5. Even if you are sure you know God's will for another person, should you pressure or manipulate him to do God's will? What will happen if you do?

6. Do you or others have preconceived ideas as to what kind(s) of a vocation a totally yielded person should pursue?

7. Within the marriage situation, to what extent is God's will personal and different from His will for one's spouse? If we make allowances for His will being different in our mate's life, will it lead to division and separation?

8. Is there a time to yield to the wishes of a group or should we always "do our own thing"? Should we at times yield even if we believe it is not God's perfect will? Explain how and when.

9. Nehemiah (2:9) had troops to protect him whereas Ezra (8:21–23) felt it was inconsistent with his testimony. How do you reconcile the difference?

7
GOD'S WILL IS PROGRESSIVE

Many people seeking God's will are looking for a blueprint—but God doesn't give out any. They are looking for a master plan outlining the details of their entire life, especially where they are going to live, in what profession they will be, and whom they will marry. Though God may reveal some distant outlines of the shape of our life to come, for the most part His will is revealed in the now. He gives us enough insight into the future to set a course, but our day-by-day walk within His will is more like a scroll than a blueprint. A scroll is rolled on two sticks. If you want to read the scroll you unroll a little on the right stick as you roll up a little on the left. Things get all messed up if you unroll the entire scroll.

So it is with our lives. We see just the now for the most part. If we try to look too far into the future, we may blow the whole thing. As stated earlier, Isaiah 28:13 says God's will is "precept upon precept, precept upon precept, line upon line, line upon line." God's will for tomorrow builds upon God's will fulfilled in our lives today. The children of Israel had to step out in their journey to the Promised Land before many doors were opened. A map ahead of time of their course to the Promised Land would not have made sense. In 1 Kings 17:1–9 God directed Elijah first to hide himself at the brook Cherith and there God fed him by means of ravens. Later He told Elijah to go to Zarephath and there a widow gave him food. Two different locations—two different means of sustenance. The second means was only revealed after the first was totally exhausted. Abraham "went out, not knowing where he was to go" (Hebrews 11:8). It was an act of faith, for he had no idea where God would lead him. Likewise we must be willing to take one step at a time, to take the first step before we know where the next step will be.

Some of us want to have the whole blueprint revealed before we start, because we either don't want to trust Him day by day, or we want to decide if it's what we want to get involved with (*see* Exodus 16:4). We have the attitude Lord, You tell me Your will and I will tell You if I want to do it. However, this attitude indicates that we have not made Him Lord; therefore, we probably never will know His will. He reveals His will when we need to know it. Rarely does He show the details of His will ahead of time. Cornelius had to be obedient to God's will so far as it was revealed before God sent more light (*see* Acts 10).

When it comes right down to it, there are so many uncertainties in life we never know what a day may bring. And it's often just as well we don't. The day may start out perfectly, but before it is over a fender is banged, a loved one is in the hospital, an unexpected crisis occurs at work, or we might even experience our graduation to heaven.

Sometimes when we know the end we have to be careful that we don't rush in or try to push God. When David was told that he was going to be king, he was very careful not to accelerate God's plan, even though he was encouraged by His associates to do so, and possibly had a right to do so (*see* 1 Samuel 24). *The end never justifies the means.* Abraham learned that to hurry God's appointed will leads to tremendous problems. God promised him an heir. After waiting patiently for ten years he took matters into his own hands and had a child by his wife's maid. He failed to wait the additional thirteen years, when his wife would have a son though she was ninety and Abraham one hundred years of age. Man's premature intervention created a lot of heartache for everyone (*see* Genesis 15:2–6; 16; 17:15–19).

God doesn't always lead us in the most direct manner. An example is recorded in Exodus 13:17, 18 of the Living Bible. God deliberately led the Israelites on a longer route because He "felt the people might become discouraged by having to fight their way through" the shorter path.

God's will is also progressive in the sense that He requires more of us as we grow. Exodus 17:1 tells us that God led the Israelites by "stages." A good example of this is in Exodus 14, when God parted the Red Sea. He allowed a wind to dry up the water all night long before their eyes. Then He told them to walk out on the dry land which they could clearly see. There was hardly any need of faith in this action. But as the children of Israel walked farther on their road with God, He expected more maturity, faith, and obedience. The next time they needed to cross a body of water, the Jordan River, the priests were required to put their feet into the water before the waters parted (*see* Exodus 14:21, 22; Joshua 3:13).

I have been endeavoring to know and follow God's will for about thirty years. I have learned a lot in the process but I find that knowing and doing His will today is still the full-time job that it was thirty years ago. It takes all the ability, all the resources, and all the relying on Christ of which I am capable.

Romans 12:2 says, in Phillips's translation "Prove in practice" God's will. The thought here is that as we grow we test it, or try (prove) it in our step-by-step endeavor to follow Him. Ephesians 5:10 puts it this way: "Learn as you go along what pleases the Lord" (LB). Early in our Christian experience His Word is very explicit in what He wants us to do. Accept Christ, stop the overt sins, fellowship with other believers, study God's Word. Then as we grow, the finer decisions, the more difficult ones, start taking place, which require that we "prove in practice" God's will. Remember Psalms 32:8, 9: "I will instruct thee and teach thee in the way which thou shalt go: I will guide thee with mine eye. Be not as the horse, or as the mule, which have no understanding: whose mouth must be held in with bit and bridle, lest they come near unto thee" (KJV). God will instruct us, but He may do it with only the movement of His eye. When we are sensitive to Him we will know His leading. We should not be like the mule, which must be forced with bit and bridle to travel a certain course. God will never force us to follow His will.

QUESTIONS

1. If God's will is mainly in the now and He doesn't give out blueprints, why shouldn't we just concentrate on living for God now and totally forget the future?

2. Do you believe the end ever justifies the means? in God's work? in your secular work?

3. As you look back on your life, can you now see why God did not reveal all of His will to you the first time you sought His guidance? Give a specific example.

4. If the children of Israel had expected God to always dry up the water before they were required to move, what would have happened? What are the implications for us? Can you give an example in your life when it has been necessary to step out by faith? Do you believe "stepping out by faith" is ever overused or misused? Explain.

8

GOD'S WILL IS DYNAMIC

God's will is dynamic and, within certain limits, alterable. You may reply that is heresy since we have a changeless God who knows the end from the beginning (*see* Malachi 3:6). Being God He has no reason to change. Humans change but never God. In fact, we are reminded in Hebrews 6:17 that even His purposes are unchangeable. Ephesians 1:5 tells us of "His unchanging plan" (LB). His Word further states, "For truly, I say to you, till heaven and earth pass away, not an iota, not a dot, will pass from the law until all is accomplished" (Matthew 5:18). For years Christian leaders have taught us this. A. W. Tozer, whose writings I highly respect, says in *The Knowledge of the Holy*, "God never changes

. . . neither does He change His mind about anything." There-fore, much of Christendom has been firmly convinced that noth-ing about God can change.

I would agree that most things that have to do with God are not changeable. Christ Himself, despite His prayer and agony, could not change the mind of God in the Garden of Gethsemane because this was God's one and only plan of salvation and re-demption for mankind. God's character, His love, the fact of sin and that its penalty must be paid, His basic timetable, are a few of the unchangeables. To alter these would be to change God and His declared Word. Regarding God Himself, His declared truths and promises, we are assured "The Lord has sworn and will never change his mind" (Hebrews 7:21 LB). But to conclude from this that His will regarding details of our lives *never* changes, in my opinion, is error. This causes many sincere Christians difficul-ties in understanding God's will.

God's will is, in fact, dynamic, not static. It may seem to change, or it may, in fact, actually change. Let's look for a moment at situations where it may seem to change. Of course, if we were wrong in the first place as to what we thought God's will was, then it may seem to change. Actually, of course, this is no change in God's plan, it is just our willingness to see and admit that we were wrong all the time. I include this, though, because I think it is a fairly common occurrence. We may ill-advisedly come to a con-clusion as to what God's will is, march ahead along that path, get ourselves in trouble, and then face the dilemma of admitting we were wrong to ourselves and others (*see* 2 Kings 5:10–14).

Many people pathetically persist out of God's will because consciously or subconsciously they are unwilling to admit that they were wrong and thus hurt their image. Thus they persist out of His will—maybe "doing God's work"—and suffer as a conse-quence. Many times "what people will think" is a strong deter-rent keeping us from God's will. It takes a fairly big person to be willing to admit that he was wrong and to start anew. But that is what we need to do—and do as quickly as we recognize the situation, moving ahead in God's perfect will for our lives.

Another situation when God's plan may seem to change is in His testing or proving us (*see* Deuteronomy 8:2–5). He may have to occasionally allow testing to see if our desire to please Him is greater than our desire to hold on to a promise or plan that He has given us. Abraham had to be willing to totally yield his greatest possession—Isaac—who embodied both God's and Abraham's hope for the future. God had no intent of actually taking Isaac's life, but only wanted to clarify what was most important to Abraham. The rich young ruler had to be willing to give up his most precious possession—his riches. He wasn't willing so he never found out anything more about God's will for his life. So far as we know he remained sorrowful the rest of his life. He never found out if God would permanently require this of him or if perchance twice as much would be returned to him, as was the case with Job.

Another way that God's will or plan may seem to change is if we read into His plan far more than He initially intended. We may assume things that He never told us. These are often things for which we hope. Let me illustrate. I live in a suburb of Los Angeles, and a short distance from us is the San Diego Freeway. If, on a given day, I believe God wants me to head south on the San Diego Freeway, I might well assume that I am to go all the way to San Diego, 125 miles down the road. However, the direction given is only to head south on the San Diego Freeway. The destination might be Long Beach, just 10 miles away. If I do not remain sensitive I can easily miss the turnoff, become confused, uneasy, and perhaps anxious, because I read into the directions far more than was intended. So it can be in our walk with God.

God's will is dynamic to the point where it may, in fact, actually change. If we deny God this right, we not only limit Him, but we also misunderstand His character and create confusion for ourselves and others in understanding His will for our lives (*see* 1 Chronicles 21:15 LB). I believe this is well supported by carefully reading God's Word. Admittedly it may not occur very often. But it is an inevitable and necessary result of His allowing us to act as free agents with our own wills, the option of choice, and self-determination within certain prescribed bounds (*see* Jeremiah 18:9, 10 LB; 1 Samuel 2:30, 31 LB).

God, in fact, changes His plan at times to see if we are more stuck on the plan than the Planner. The first time God provided a miraculous supply of water in the desert, Moses was specifically commanded to strike the rock. The desired result: water gushed forth. The second time Moses, possibly frustrated and irate over the disobedience of the Israelites, either wasn't listening carefully or ignored God's direction. Although instructed to take his rod and *speak* to the rock (*see* Numbers 20:8–12), Moses *struck* the rock as he had done the first time, instead of merely speaking to it. He struck the rock twice and God gave water the second time, even though striking the rock was an act of disobedience. Moses didn't lose any stature before his followers in this situation but he certainly did with God, because it prevented his entering the Promised Land, God's initial plan for Moses. Being stuck on a method, more than the Maker, got him into trouble.

Another example of the Israelites' getting stuck on a method was their use of the serpent. Initially the serpent was God's method of deliverance for stricken Israelites. Later they worshiped the serpent and it became a sin (*see* Numbers 21:5–9; 2 Kings 18:4). The Israelites were typical of all of us who tend to get so wrapped up in methods and means that we lose sight of Him. Elijah's being fed by two different means is also an example of God changing methods. The writer of Hebrews puts it succinctly: "So we can plainly see that God's method changed" (Hebrews 7:15 LB).

God's will may change due to lack of obedience. In Mark 10:2–6 God changed the divorce laws. Admittedly this was because of the hardness of the individuals' hearts. Nevertheless, there was a change. In Numbers 14 we find that one day the children of Israel were commanded to fight against their enemy, but they disobeyed. The next day, though their enemy was still unbeaten, they were commanded not to fight. Although they admitted they had sinned, Moses warned them, "It's too late. Now you are disobeying the Lord's orders to return to the wilderness" (verse 41 LB). Despite this they engaged in battle and failed. Sin prevented Moses from entering into God's Promised Land and it delayed God's plan for the children of Israel (*see* Exodus 3:7–12; Numbers 20:8–25; Deuteronomy 1:34–38).

God's will may also change due to obedience. When the people of Nineveh changed, God in love changed His plan regarding their destruction. This change affected a third party, Jonah. Unfortunately he was rigid and unwilling to accept this dynamic change in God's will.

Intercessory prayer can also change God's plan and will. Moses forcefully interceded for the children of Israel: "So the Lord changed his mind and spared them" (Exodus 32:14 LB; *see also* Psalms 106:23). Christ, seeing the need and distress of the disciples in the storm, altered His intended course and responded to them in their distress (*see* Mark 6:45–52).

Why make such a big point of all of this? It is to warn that we must not lose sight of God, despite all of our wonderful plans, programs, methods, strategies, and goals. We must remain sensitive and open to God's instant leading, so that we can be like Philip, who was successful in what he was doing but was whisked away by the Spirit for a new opportunity (*see* Acts 8:29).

God's will is dynamic, flexible, and at times unpredictable. However, we can be assured He will guide us hand in hand through whatever course He intends for us. If we want His blessing, either as individuals or in the corporate fellowship of the church, we must be in constant union with Him, carefully listening lest we miss our fork in the road. We can never smugly rest on yesterday's relationship or leading.

However, let me caution that I don't think we need to be morbidly introspective for fear we might miss the turn in the road. This would be like planting a garden and every day going out and digging it up to see how it is doing. If God directs us to do something we can proceed in doing that. Then, as we are daily waiting on Him and open to Him, He will direct us if we should change our course. Let me warn you, however, that we must be sure it is the *Lord* who has changed our direction. The man of God was led astray by the prophet of God, who informed him that God had changed His will for his life (*see* 1 Kings 13). But the prophet lied and because of it the man of God lost his life. It all comes back to being obedient in the present and listening carefully to our Master's voice. He most assuredly wants to reveal His will to us. All we have to do is listen.

QUESTIONS

1. Traditional Christianity repeatedly has emphasized that we have an unchangeable God. Placing emphasis on the fact that God's plan is dynamic may seem to run counter to traditional Christianity. Do you see a conflict? What do you really believe? What problems can develop with an overemphasis on either side of this issue?

2. How does the doctrine of foreknowledge and predestination apply to this chapter?

3. Some things are unchangeable, some are not. List the key things that God reassures us are unchangeable, those things that comfort and give spiritual and emotional stability to the person in His will.

4. Should we ever try to change God's mind? What is the danger in this?

9
YOUR DESIRES AND GOD'S WILL

If it's fun—it must be wrong. If it's what you want to do—it's pretty clear it's not going to be what God wants. If you are really surrendered—you will be suffering for Christ. If you are willing to go anywhere—it's obvious He will send you to the place you detest most. God's will, in essence, will always run counter to what you hold most dear. As a young Christian I was often plagued with a haunting thought. If I really yielded my life to God He would send me to the worst corner of the world as a missionary and have me marry a girl I didn't want to marry.

These erroneous thought patterns permeate deeply into Christianity and, in fact, often keep non-Christians from God. It's one of Satan's big lies. If we don't hear it preached from our pulpits it's often implied. It's so deeply ingrained that many Christians feel guilty if they enjoy something. Many Christians have had their desires stifled so long that they don't know themselves or their desires, which is unfortunate. (I am aware of the Scripture teachings on "dying daily" and the other extreme that would make everything unrealistically easy. I am not promoting either of these extremes, so please hear me out.)

We often feel that to have any desires or wishes of our own is wrong. It seems to me that some have advocated annihilation of our desires to truly know and live God's will.

George Müller of Bristol once said, "I get my heart into such a state that it has no will of its own in the matter." "Seek to have no will of your own," he advised, "in order to ascertain the mind of God regarding any steps you propose to take. . . ." He seems to be saying we must annihilate our own wills and desires in order to know God's will for our lives.

I hesitate to differ with a great man like Müller who undoubtedly walked close to God and no doubt pleased God more than I do. However, I am not convinced that God's prerequisite for knowing His will is the total annihilation of our desires. Elisabeth Elliot, in her excellent book *A Slow And Certain Light,* points out that Christ in the Garden of Gethsemane had a marked conflict because He preferred His own personal desire of avoiding the cross. Nevertheless, He was willing to submit His desire to God. He was willing to say, "Not my will, but thine, be done" (Luke 22:42).

Abraham is another example. He loved his son dearly and I am sure he longed for Isaac's deliverance even though he was set to kill him. I don't think there was ever a moment when Abraham's desire for Isaac's life was ever annihilated. Nevertheless, *that necessary element, the total yielding of that desire to God, was present.* There are many other examples in the Scriptures of saints whose desires were clearly different from God's and yet they were willing to yield them to the Father.

The Scriptures teach that *our desires have a place within God's will.* Matthew 7 speaks of the person who seeks and finds, and verse 11 says, "And if you hardhearted, sinful men know how to give good gifts to your children, won't your Father in heaven even more certainly give good gifts to those who ask him for them?" (LB).

Psalms 37:4 says, "Be delighted with the Lord. Then *he will give you all your heart's desires"* (LB author's italics). Psalms 145:19 states, *"He fulfills the desires* of those who reverence and trust him" (LB author's italics). And Proverbs 10:24 says, ". . . but *the desire of the righteous will be granted"* (author's italics). However, with many of these verses prerequisites are implied.

Solomon is a good example of some of these principles. God gave Solomon the free choice to ask whatever he would. He could easily have asked for the things that we usually desire: wealth, fame, prestige, or power. Instead Solomon chose those things which were closer to God's heart—the ability to judiciously rule God's people. God was pleased with this request and not only gave Solomon his request but also added the more human desires. Thus, as we walk closer to God our desires and His more closely mesh. We are more likely to fulfill His desires, and in the process be allowed some of the things we deeply desire.

However, *it must be clearly emphasized that our desires and will must always be yielded to God.* The desire of the rich young ruler was, in fact, idolatry (*see* Matthew 19:16–22). His desire for riches was more important to him than God and this desire kept him from the kingdom of God. If our desires involve frank sin they obviously must be dealt with accordingly. When we first come to Christ and our life has been in sin many of our desires are going to have to be "crucified" if we are going to walk with Him (*see* Galatians 5:17–24; Ephesians 2:3). Even after we have been Christians for a longer period of time our fleshly desires keep cropping up and we must boldly deal with them. If our desires are not sinful in themselves, they still must be yielded to God. We must come to the place where we say, "It's okay, God, if You don't want this for me, I will follow Your will. In fact, I most definitely want Your will, even though it is contrary to my human desires." In this sense I think Müller's emphasis is correct. If our desire is contrary to God's will, His will is so much more important that our desire doesn't make any difference. We are willing to submit it totally to God, knowing His will is best for us in the long run.

As we voluntarily yield our desire to His will, several things happen. First, we slowly become aware that what He wants for us is really what's best for us after all. Those things which we desired in the past would not, in the final analysis, have satisfied the deep longings of our heart. The things that He desires for us do satisfy the deep longings of our heart.

Second, we will start to find that our desires are beginning to mesh with His desires. As we see things with the spiritual insight God gives us, values will change (*see* Romans 10:1). Third, as we become more mature we will be able to cautiously trust our desires. We will realize that our loving heavenly Father is interested in our desires and wants to fulfill many of them that are within His will (*see* Nehemiah 2:18).

Hannah Whitall Smith says in *The Christian's Secret of a Happy Life:*

> God's promise is that He will work in us to *will* as well as to do of His good pleasure. This means, of course, that He will take possession of our will, and work it for us; and that His suggestions will come to us, not so much commands from the outside as desires springing up within. They will originate in our will; we shall feel as though we *desired* to do so and so, not as though we *must*. And this makes it a service of perfect liberty; for it is always easy to do what we desire to do, let the accompanying circumstances be as difficult as they may. . . . We are *drawn* to obey instead of being driven to it.

> The way in which the Holy Spirit, therefore, usually works, in a fully obedient soul, in regard to this direct guidance, is to impress upon the mind a wish or desire to do or to leave undone certain things.

Fourth, certain choices within His perfect will are entirely up to us. This may be because He holds us *responsible* for making the decision (*see* chapters 4, 18, and 19) or because He is giving us the *privilege* of doing what we would like to do—of course—within His perfect will.

Regarding choices that are ours: You probably would agree with me that at least some of the time He may not care about what color you paint your house, or the make of automobile you purchase. It may at times include such far-reaching things as our occupation, the city we live in, or the person we marry. This is not to say, however, that God isn't concerned about the choice. It may be very similar to a parent's feelings about a son or daughter getting married. A good parent will positively look forward to the time when his offspring will be mature and ready for a beautiful marriage. The parent will not pick out the spouse for the son or daughter but naturally will have some ideals for that person. Within these ideals the son or daughter has complete freedom to seek and decide on a mate. At times God's will may be like that.

My wife likes to illustrate this point by referring to the three areas of God's will mentioned earlier: His perfect will, His permissive will, and the area outside His will. Many possible choices can be made within each area. Our target with its bull's-eye illustrates this. There are numerous points within the bull's-eye —an arrow landing anywhere within that circle is a bull's-eye and an equally perfect hit. Let's use the example of a fellow considering marriage. It is possible that Joe could marry either one of two girls within God's perfect will and any one of four girls within His permissive will and an infinite number of girls outside of His will. This is illustrated below:

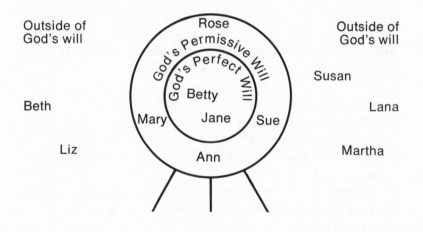

Paul Little, in his book *Affirming the Will of God,* quotes A. W. Tozer as saying that we should not seek God's guidance for things that He has already forbidden, nor for things about which He has already given us a specific command, but that in most other things God has no preference. John MacArthur, Jr. in *God's Will Is Not Lost* says that after you have met certain conditions, the next principle of God's will is "Do whatever you want!" Centuries ago Saint Augustine said, "Love God and do whatever you want." The chapter on guidance (written under the pseudonym of Christopher Ford) in the book *I Wish I Had Known* tells us, "Walk with God as best you know how, do what you really want to do, and don't let anyone stop you. Does that sound dangerous? It is. Does it sound very 'unspiritual'? It is not. Does it sound terribly simple? Well, that can fool you, but it is quite simple."

Admittedly *statements like this must be carefully qualified* or they will be abused and one will end up outside of God's will. Nevertheless, I think it is important to realize that *in some situations the choice may be ours, probably in a lot more situations than many of us sincere, dedicated Christians imagine.* If God has given us the right to choose, we may become confused if we keep looking to Him for an answer that He is never going to give. Therefore, when we have done all the other things discussed in this book and it appears that God is leaving the choice up to us—decide, using your God-enlightened insight. Consider whether or not one of the choices available is more likely to please Him and bring glory to His Name—if so, choose that. Otherwise *make the choice you want within God's perfect will.* You need not fret, worry, or stall in indecision. Love God and do whatever you want. The realization of what this means can be wonderfully liberating.

QUESTIONS

1. Do you agree that one should totally annihilate his own desires, or that this isn't necessary? Explain why. What precautions are indicated with either position?

2. George Müller was a saint of God, used mightily for the kingdom of God. How do you feel about questioning something a person like this says? Should we ever question spiritual leaders of this day? Is there a right and wrong way to do it? Describe.

3. Do you agree that *at times* it may be up to an individual where he lives, what profession he is in, and whom he marries? If, for example, it is up to us whom we marry, does that mean we can marry anyone we wish? Do you think it is possible that God has *only one person* within His will for a given individual to marry?

4. Do you think God ever allows us total free choice to prove what is in our heart like He did with Solomon? What are the ramifications of the choices that we make in such a situation?

*5. If you could ask God for any one thing and be assured ahead of time that He would give it to you, what would you ask of Him?

*6. How do you internally picture God?

    (a) a killjoy or scrooge

    (b) a hard taskmaster

    (c) far off and uninterested in you

    (d) a Father who is deeply concerned about your well-being and desires

    (e) other: List _____

7. I know a world-renowned Christian leader who was asked by two churches in different cities to speak to them on the same night. Both requesting churches added that they had prayed about it and were convinced it was God's will that he come to their church that night. Neither knew of the other group's request. I remember the Christian leader telling us that one of the groups had to be out of God's will. What do you think?

8. A Christian patient I know had to choose a physician for a difficult medical problem. She prayerfully evaluated and honestly concluded that Dr. A should be the one she should see. She told me: "I am sure this is God's will." However, Dr. A didn't feel he could handle her problem and advised her to seek an-

other physician. This created a real problem for the patient. There are many possible explanations as to why this occurred. However, do you think we often get confused in this sort of a situation because we think of God's will as only one possible course of action (Dr. A) instead of realizing that in many situations there may be several courses of action (Drs. A, B, and D) within God's perfect will? If that is the case would it have been more accurate for the patient to have said, "I believe it's within God's will for me to see Dr. A"? This does not exclude the later possibility of seeing Drs. B or D or confusion when Dr. A says no.

9. I know a girl who received marriage proposals from three different men. Each was a sincere and dedicated Christian and each told her he believed it was God's will that she marry him. How would you explain this? Was only one correct? What should the girl do?

10. Regarding choices equally in God's perfect will, one Christian writer says, "Choose the harder of the two ways," as opposed to the one that you desire. What are the reasons for and against each of these approaches and the long-term implications of each?

10
YOUR ABILITIES AND GOD'S WILL

As God's messenger I give each of you God's warning: Be honest in your estimate of yourselves, measuring your value by how much faith God has given you. Just as there are many parts to our bodies, so it is with Christ's body. We are all part of it, and it takes every one of us to make it complete, for we each have different work to do. So we belong to each other, and each needs all the others.

God has given each of us the ability to do certain things well. So if God has given you the ability to prophesy, then prophesy whenever you can—as often as your faith is strong enough to receive a message from God. If your gift is that of serving others, serve them well. If you are a teacher, do a good job of teaching. If you are a preacher, see to it that your sermons are strong and helpful. If God has given you money, be generous in helping others with it. If God has given you administrative ability and put you in charge of the work of others, take the responsibility seriously. Those who offer comfort to the sorrowing should do so with Christian cheer.

Romans 12:3–8 LB author's italics

It is important for us to honestly evaluate our God-given abilities. Generally, I believe God's will or plan for our lives follows these abilities rather closely. We read in 1 Corinthians 7:7 that "each has his own special gift from God." I believe as we yield our lives to God we will learn where our talents or abilities lie, and under His grace those areas in our lives will blossom. However, finding our abilities occasionally involves the willingness to try new things.

We also must be open to the occasional exception when God may choose to use us despite our inability in a given area. Moses was chosen by God to be His spokesman, not only to the children of Israel but also to the ruling Egyptians (*see* Exodus 4:10–14; Jeremiah 1:6–19). Moses, looking only at his inabilities in this particular area, repeatedly questioned God's desire to use a self-effacing person like himself. But God greatly used this insecure, timid man as a mighty leader. David was no match for Goliath. Gideon's small army had no chance against the giant army of the Midianites. But these and numerous other accounts in the Scriptures show how God can take that which is weak and incapable and make it into something of significance and usefulness to Him.

In each situation when abilities do not match the job ordained by God, He makes it exceedingly clear either with a supernatural revelation or by a very deep assurance within the individual that this is God's will (*see* Exodus 3, 4; Judges 6; 1 Samuel 17:24–47).

In general, I believe God usually leads us into areas where we have already proven some degree of effectiveness. If you believe God is leading you into a work, position, or calling—evaluate whether or not you have the abilities needed for such a pursuit. If you don't know, ask for help from an appropriate friend, minister, or counselor. Vocational testing may be of help to some people. "Try your hand" in a limited way. God was willing to first prove in a small way, to Moses and Gideon alone, that He would give the ability. So, if you feel called to the ministry, speak to some small groups, teach some Bible classes and the like. There should be an increasing ability, desire, and measure of success in most instances if it's of God that you go into that area of ministry. Before you obligate yourself to a lifelong commitment, try to get some experience when possible. For example, my brother Paul had been interested for years in medical missions and wondered if this was God's calling. After completing all of his training he went to Zaire (formerly the Congo) as a missionary doctor for a limited commitment. During those four months God completely assured him that this was where he should invest his life.

If you find you don't have God-given abilities, effectiveness, and a deep desire in the area into which He is calling you—you had better be very sure He is doing the calling. However, you can be assured that He has given you some ability that will be fulfilling to you and will glorify Him.

QUESTIONS

1. Are our abilities, talents, and spiritual gifts such as are mentioned in 1 Corinthians 12, 13, and 14 the same? Are they ever different? Explain.

*2.   Do you believe every Christian has some special ability or gift for the kingdom of God? What is yours? Can you have more than one gift?

3.   If one is not aware of his ability or gift, how does he find out what it is?

4.   How might other people be agents in helping us find our God-given abilities? When might people be a problem to us along this line?

5.   Do you think that people are ever pressed into some specific full-time Christian work who don't have that God-given ability? Why does this happen?

6.   Which do you think is more common:

(a) Christians doing jobs they don't have the ability or God's call to do, or

(b) Christians with the ability and call who are undiscovered or idle?

11
NEEDS AND GOD'S WILL

Seldom do humans overhear God speak. When they do—what do they hear? The Prophet Isaiah heard God say, "Whom shall I send, and who will go for us?" (Isaiah 6:8). God's concern was for the spiritual needs of His people and He was questioning who would be His human instrument to help meet that need. Fortunately Isaiah responded. Later in the Scriptures we find a different situation in which God found no one who was willing to be His instrument of righteousness to help others in need (*see* Ezekiel 22:30).

Throughout the Scriptures we find God's great concern for

mankind and its needs. Christ's coming to earth not only typifies this great concern for our needs but His life is also the epitome of it. The Scriptures say:

> And what pity He felt for the crowds that came, because their problems were so great and they didn't know what to do or where to go for help. They were like sheep without a shepherd. "The harvest is so great, and the workers are so few," he told his disciples. "So pray to the one in charge of the harvesting, and ask him to recruit more workers for his harvest fields."
>
> Matthew 9:36–38LB

Christ's concern for mankind included not only spiritual needs but emotional and physical needs as well. The closer we are to God the more we become aware of God's concern for individual and worldwide needs. Christ expressed this concern to His disciples, after they had been with Him some three years, when He said, "As the Father has sent me, even so I send you" to meet the spiritual needs of people (John 20:21). This was His last command to the disciples (*see* Matthew 28:18,19).

We also find that the closer we are to people the more we become aware of their needs and God puts within us a greater desire to meet those needs. So, *the person who would know God's will for his life must consider the needs of the world around him.* We must remain very aware that He is "not willing that any should perish, but that all should come to repentance" (2 Peter 3:9 KJV; *see also* John 6:29 LB). God probably will want to use us in some way to get out the good news of His love. If we are going to be living in His will we must be aware of the needs and open to how God wants us to meet those needs.

However, the need is not necessarily the call. So often we hear of mind-staggering needs from pulpiteers, mail appeals, even from manipulating friends. These high-pressure presentations leave us with the feeling that the need necessitates our action. In my opinion, however, the need never in itself necessitates action. The need is only one of many considerations in deciding whether or not we should fulfill that need. This is true even if it means that some needs may go unmet.

Many people are driven by the tyranny of needs. By trying to meet too many needs, they often become insensitive to their own legitimate needs, the legitimate needs of their family and others close to them. Ultimately they become insensitive to God as they are driven by "needs." It is not even unusual for these same people to become insensitive to the real hurts of the people to whom they are trying to minister. (For further discussion along this line read chapters 14, 16, 17, 18, and 21 in *Run and Not Be Weary* by the author.)

Christ was not always led by needs. In Luke 5:15, 16 we find that ". . . great multitudes gathered to hear and to be healed of their infirmities. But he withdrew to the wilderness and prayed." And in another place Christ reprimanded His disciples for thinking that all money should be utilized for the needs of the poor. He, in fact, rebuked them by saying, "For you always have the poor with you . . ." (Matthew 26:11).

Take a moment and think about the years prior to Christ's ministry. No doubt many years prior to His active ministry He became aware of His power to heal and to meet the many needs around Him, yet we find Him apparently passing up all these opportunities to minister to these needs. The reason, no doubt, was the same one given in John 2:4, when He said, "I can't help you now. It isn't yet my time for miracles" (LB).

Many problems are created by pressures from well-meaning but ill-advised leaders. A leader who sees only the needs "out there" creates a new set of needs at home. It is no wonder that many great Christian leaders who are so concerned about the needs of the world end up with some gigantic needs in their own homes. I believe we must keep all needs in mind—our own and our family's as well as the world's. To do this means we must be sensitive to all these areas but we must also be listening carefully to God and His will in the matter. We can never meet all the needs of the world. We must determine which ones God wants us to meet. This is a crucial choice.

This reminds me of the many messages I heard calling for my recruitment to missionary service. I'm sure I raised my hand or went forward a score of times to "calls from beyond" for full-time missionary service. The needs were stressed, the fact that it was so much on God's heart, and the question repeatedly put to me and my peers: "Are you willing to go wherever the Lord wants you to go?" Since I truly wanted God's best, I was willing to go to the mission field or any place He should lead—and in the process I was left with the distinct impression that I should get on with things, that is, get ready for the mission field. I wrestled with this for years, looking into every aspect of it, searching my heart, and even visiting mission fields.

But then I began to look at my abilities. I not only detested foreign languages but I also got a D in my third semester of high-school French on the condition I would voluntarily drop the subject. I don't like to camp out in the United States—to say nothing of roughing it in a foreign country. I enjoy the basic American foods—not the exotic foreign ones. Now I am convinced that God could change these desires and abilities in me—but He hasn't. In fact, I was willing to go despite these things not being changed. However, I finally became aware that Christian leaders' pressure to the contrary, I could be in the center of God's will—in fact I *was* in the center of His will—and not be in a foreign country or in so-called full-time Christian work. This does not mean this is His will for you, nor does it mean it will be for me next year. All of us must be open to His leading and ready for any change. But the point is, needs alone do not determine God's perfect will for my life or yours. Only God's personal leading in your life determines His will.

In this chapter I have tried to call your attention to two sides of an issue: There is a legitimate and important aspect of being sensitive to the tremendous needs of the world, but on the other hand, we must be careful not to be driven and guided only by those needs. Unfortunately, human nature being what it is, we often pick the side that we want to hear and totally miss the other side. By presenting both sides of this issue, I may have lent support to whichever side you have chosen. My aim has not been to do that, but to help point out that there *are* two sides. I trust and pray that you will honestly evaluate both sides before God and really listen to what He is trying to say to you about needs.

QUESTIONS

1. What, in your opinion, is God's greatest concern?

2. Do you think you can meet the spiritual needs of an individual without meeting his emotional and physical needs? Can you meet the needs of others if all of your needs are not met?

3. Can you picture Christ passing by needs? Why do you think He did this?

4. Some may consider it a gloomy picture that legitimate needs will probably go unmet if they don't meet them. If every Christian did God's will, do you think all of the needs of the world would be met? Why doesn't God intervene and meet the needs?

5. Why do you think Christian leaders emphasize "the need" so much? I have heard it said that "the opportunity plus ability equals the responsibility." Is this correct?

6. Do you think many of the problems we find in the church and at home are because we have overstressed the needs outside the church and have not adequately dealt with our own needs first? Have you been affected by this? How?

7. Have you ever felt that the only way to be completely in God's perfect will is to be a missionary or in some other full-time work? Do you still feel that way?

8. Do you think we ought to meet all the needs of our family and children before we try to meet any needs outside the family?

12
HUMAN AUTHORITY AND GOD'S WILL

Recently my wife and I had dinner with a dear couple who both came to know the Lord through a certain church almost twenty years ago. They were married in the church and all of their means of spiritual growth came through that church and its pastor. They were appreciative and felt indebted to this body of believers.

In the process they were taught that they had to attend all the church meetings if they were completely yielded to Christ. Even though he had to get up at half-past three in the morning and often work as many as twelve hours a day, he was expected to attend church virtually all day Sunday and three nights a week. He was taught that the source of truth was, of course, God's Word and he should spend an hour a day in it, and spend one to two hours per day in prayer. In addition, the minister of that church considered himself God's agent to reveal God's will to the congregation. They were not to listen to Christian radio stations or outside Christian speakers or even read Christian books, except maybe their own Sunday-school quarterly.

Needless to say, as the years passed the couple became very weary, legalistic Christians wanting to please God, but finding that they and their friends had bigger hang-ups than they had before they accepted Christ. They couldn't talk with others within the group or even to each other about what was really going on in their lives. They could only talk about "Jesus." It was a rude awakening when they learned that their leaders were normal human beings, unable to fully decide God's will for others. This didn't happen in some monastery or in a foreign country, but in the "good old U.S.A." and within a church that may look a lot like yours or mine. Fortunately, these extreme cases are not too common, but more subtle examples of Christians exercising lordship over others is ubiquitous (*see* Mark 10:42–45; Luke 22:24–27; 1 Peter 5:1–5).

Spiritual domination like this is, I believe, the inevitable result when we overstress human authority. Some teach "the chain of command" and if this is practiced to its full implication without qualification, it can also lead to human domination. The chain of command is the teaching that Christians should be subject to their parents, to their youth director, to their pastor, to their government, with a sort of blind allegiance. It is a military term. How well I remember my experience in boot camp when the chain of command was explained to me. There was never the remotest suggestion that I could question an order.

Recent world events have made it clear that society will not buy the blind obedience of followers to its leaders. This is illustrated not only by the trials of Hitler's subordinates but also more recently in our own Watergate trials. I believe the Scriptures clearly teach that we should never *blindly* obey men—no matter how spiritual they may seem. Nevertheless, we who are in the church or other Christian organizations are often encouraged to have such an allegiance. We sometimes are taught that if we question what is said, we are blatantly questioning what God is saying. A leader's will is interpreted as God's will.

Why do some people demand such allegiance in the name of Christianity? I think the answers are easy to see. First of all, it allows a lot of control over one's subordinates. Second, it appears to make life a lot safer, more predictable and controllable. On the surface it seems to simplify life. When you make everything black or white it allows people to "get on with the job." Unfortunately, however, life is not that simple. Eventually emotional and spiritual growth will be stifled and the results will be devastating. (For further discussion on this point read chapter 16, "The Urge to Make and Become Followers" in *Run and Not Be Weary* by the author.)

But, you quickly inject, doesn't God's Word command that we "Obey them that have the rule over you, and submit yourselves . . ." (*see* Hebrews 13:17 KJV)? Certainly the Scriptures are filled with commands that we should be subject to certain people, leaders, and our government, even when its decisions may not be the best. The Bible also tells us to obey our employers (*see* Ephesians 6:5–7 and Colossians 3:22). Every husband who has been around the church for any length of time knows that wives are to be in submission to their husbands (*see* Colossians 3:18; Ephesians 5:22; 1 Peter 3:1–6). And husbands are to love their wives as Christ loved the church—no small task. Children are to be obedient to their parents (*see* Colossians 3:20; Ephesians 6:1). The head of the household is to be responsible for supporting his household and those who are dependent upon him (*see* 1 Timothy 5:8). Followers are to be obedient to their spiritual leaders. In fact, Ephesians 5:21 says that *all of us must be willing to be subject one to another.*

The Scriptures are clear on these points and those who emphasize obeying individuals in authority are on solid ground. *God usually expects us to submit in these situations. This is the rule.* As a result He *may* expect us to do things that we don't completely understand. We *may* have to do things with which we don't entirely agree. At times we *may* have to do things in a less effective way than we otherwise would have done them. In fact, we may have to do things quite differently than we would do if the relationship requiring our submission did not exist. But because of the relationship, God will often have us do certain things in obedience to people and thus to Him. And He wants us to do these things without a grudging attitude, but cheerfully as unto Him (*see* Colossians 3:22–24 and Ephesians 6:5–7).

However, as with most rules, there may be the *rare* place for an exception. *God never wants us to blindly follow and obey those who exercise authority over us. It is appropriate at times to question.* The man of God described in 1 Kings 13, as discussed earlier, learned this the hard way by blindly believing and accepting the recommendations of a religious leader. The disciples rightfully disobeyed worldly authorities by saying, "Whether it is right in the sight of God to listen to you," the religious authorities who had secular power, "rather than to God, you must judge; for we cannot but speak of what we have seen and heard" (Acts 4:19, 20).

But let me hasten to add that I am not trying to cause mutiny among Christians. I am not in any sense trying to encourage a breakdown of proper authority, submission, or relationships. But I am emphasizing this side of the point because there is a segment of Christianity that does not hear it. Failing to see the exceptions in some rules can keep sincere people from knowing God's wonderful will for their lives. Again, as in several previous chapters, I have tried to emphasize both sides of a point. Hopefully, you will properly see which side is applicable in your situation and you will be obedient to that.

Sometimes when there is a conflict regarding submission to an authority, there is an opportunity for a divinely ordained *imaginative alernative.* Daniel chose such an alternative (*see* Daniel 1:8–16). He believed the king's rich food and alcohol was not in his best interest, so he got the king's steward to agree to a ten-day trial on a more conventional diet. Daniel proved his point to the steward. By doing this, he was allowed to eat what he felt was best and still be obedient to authority. While many times there are imaginative alternatives, such alternatives are never guaranteed. Daniel eventually had to refuse to bow down to a false god as ordered by the king. Not only did he have to be willing to refuse to be obedient to a legal authority but he also had to be willing to die as a consequence of this refusal. There was no imaginative alternative available.

All of these factors should cause us to be very careful about our voluntarily accepting a situation which necessitates submission to some other human being or organization. We should be very sure it is of God. If there is any hesitancy, the advice in 1 Corinthians 7:20 is appropriate. It reads, "Every one should remain in the state in which he was called."

Therefore, always obey all rightful authority—except when you are very, very sure that a higher Authority, God, is leading you to the contrary.

QUESTIONS

1. What do you really think of the "chain of command" and its application in Christianity? Do you agree that there are rare exceptions? Is this encouraging "doing your own thing"? Can you give some examples in your own life when you felt you should be obedient to others even though it was a very difficult situation? How did you handle it?

2. Have you ever been in a position of rejecting authority and leadership? Explain what happened and whether or not you would still handle it the same way.

3. When is a person no longer responsible to his parents?

13

GOD DOESN'T WILL YOUR MISFORTUNES

A young couple who were sincere, dedicated Christians wanted God's will—His best for their lives and that of their family. They became convinced that it was God's will for their eleven-year-old boy to be cured of his illness—diabetes. Acting on faith, they stopped giving him his life-sustaining insulin. They were convinced he would be healed—but he died. They were convinced he would rise from the grave in four days—but he didn't. To all of this they said, "God led us every step of the way. We feel no sorrow, we feel no guilt. We followed God's will. He was with us. . . . It was God's will . . . but we don't understand it."

Statements such as these, in my opinion, reveal not only our lack of understanding of God's will but also how little we understand the cause of all sickness, suffering, and pain in this world.

Why there is suffering and misfortune is a universal question. How can such be God's will if God is a good God? How can there even be a God, others ask? These questions haunt Christians and non-Christians alike. Often God is used as a scapegoat for man's errant actions that cause pain and suffering.

In my opinion, GOD IS NOT RESPONSIBLE FOR THE BAD EVENTS IN THE WORLD. The misfortunes that occur are not of God's choosing or of His initial perfect will.

GOD'S VARIOUS WILLS THROUGH THE AGES

GOD'S INITIAL PERFECT WILL was to place Adam and Eve in the garden and allow them to have the joys of life forever. However, God did not want robots so he gave them free choice and the opportunity to follow Him in that perfect relationship or to disobey Him. There was only *one* condition; and if they violated it they would die (*see* Genesis 2:17; 3:1–6; Romans 6:23). *God's declared law* was death for sin. Eventually Adam and Eve transgressed. I believe God had a choice, and at that moment in time He could have killed Adam and Eve and thus annihilated the entire human race. He would have been justified in doing this. He would have doled out the proper recompense for sin. He would have resolved in a second the entire pain-and-suffering problem which has plagued humanity ever since. However, such immediate justice would have made it impossible to call out individuals who were willing to follow Him and upon whom He could pour out His love. His purpose for creating man would have been eternally frustrated and Satan would have been the victor. So God delayed His judgment for His and our sake. This, however, meant the ledger of justice and injustice would not be balanced

—for a time. Sin could be committed and its just recompense not paid—for a while.

Thus humanity entered into the AGE OF GOD'S PERMIS-SIVE WILL. Leslie D. Weatherhead, author of *The Will of God* (to whom I am indebted for stimulating some of these thoughts), calls it "The circumstantial will of God—God's plan within certain circumstances." Matthew 19:8 probably helps us understand God's feeling about this age: ". . . but it was not what God had *originally intended*" (LB author's italics). We will remain in the age of His permissive will until God chooses to stop the world as we know it and judge it, doling out to each individual his due reward. Only at this time will the ledger be balanced. Sin, wickedness, and disobedience will be paid for. However, those who have accepted Him will enter into that wonderful, endless relationship with God in heaven without pain, suffering, or injustices (*see* Revelation 21:4). When we partake of the wonderful things God has for us it will truly eclipse any brief period of trial and suffering which we had to endure during the age of His permissive will. At that time we will enter into HIS ULTIMATE WILL. This is His *re-created perfect will*. No person, wickedness, or power of Satan can prevent believers from entering into His ultimate will—the place He has prepared for those who love Him (*see* Romans 8:31–39).

THE CONSEQUENCES OF AN AGE OF GOD'S PERMISSIVE WILL

Let's look a little further at the consequences of Adam's sin. God's warning to Adam came true, though delayed, for He had said, "If you eat its fruit, you will be doomed to die" (Genesis 2:17 LB). With sin, the process of decay and deterioration, aging and death began, and continues to this day. Thus mutations of cells causing deformities, deviant cells causing cancer, and all other destructive processes and illnesses in the body *were set in motion* through Adam's sin (*compare* Matthew 6:19, 20 *with* Genesis 1:31).

Further effects of God's allowing man free choice are seen on Adam's children. Cain was jealous and though God personally encouraged him to repent he instead chose to kill his brother Abel. Now God could have intervened—just as He could have when Adam took the forbidden fruit—but if He had, we would be robots. God could have extracted just recompense from Cain after he killed his brother; He didn't, I believe, so that He might give him additional time to repent. In this incident we see another consequence of sin—that a righteous man could be hurt and killed by an angry, self-centered person. And so it continues to this day. The drunk can kill or maim a carful of innocent people. The young mother can beat her child. The rulers of nations can send their young men to the battlefields to fight and die in useless wars. God is not to be blamed for this suffering and pain. It's true that God could intervene each time we thought or did anything that was deviant—but it's His prerogative not to— probably so that you and I will have time to see the results of our acts, change our ways, and be reconciled with the Creator of the universe.

As stated earlier, during this age of God's permissive will, the ledger is not balanced. God allows the rain to fall on the just and the unjust (*see* Matthew 5:45). Were the six million Jews exterminated by Hitler more sinful than other people? Christ answered this question in Luke 13:1-5 when He told about a certain number of Jewish people who were butchered by Pilate. He told of others who had a tower fall upon them. Then He asked if those who suffered were worse than others and His answer was no. The writer of Ecclesiastes (7:15) says that he has seen the righteous perish and the wicked have prolonged life. Let's look at the saints. Many of the Old Testament prophets were killed despite their faith. Others were spared because of their faith (*see* Hebrews 11). The first Christian martyr was Stephen, a young man totally obedient to God, yet he died for his faith in Christ. In fact, eleven of the twelve apostles were martyred. If Christ's own disciples suffered so as a consequence of this sin-sick world, can we *expect* God to violate the laws of this world for us?

In rare situations He may intervene and violate the normal laws that have been set into motion. Because of the wickedness of Sodom and Gomorrah He rained fire and brimstone to destroy them (*see* Genesis 19). He occasionally may destroy an individual because of his wickedness as described in 1 Chronicles 2:3: "The oldest son, *Er,* was so wicked that the Lord killed him" (LB). Likewise the Lord may occasionally intervene to protect a righteous man from the hands of the wicked (*see* 2 Kings 6:8–19).

However, most of the time He will neither choose to violate the natural laws of nature nor to interfere with the work of unregenerated men and the resultant suffering they cause. But this is insignificant as we see the eternal perspective and realize the ledger someday will be balanced in our favor through Jesus Christ as we spend an eternity in heaven (*see* Hebrews 12:1–6).

One thing we can all be assured of is that despite any circumstance, despite any illness, any seeming misfortune, any destructive acts of men about us, there is no one but ourselves who can keep us from God's perfect will for our lives. Realizing this should cause us to rejoice in our Maker.

OTHER CAUSES OF MISFORTUNE

We have just discussed two causes for our misfortune; the sinful acts of other men and how they affect us, and the process of aging and decay which Adam and Eve set in motion. There are two other causes which should be discussed.

Before Adam sinned, one of the most honored angels in heaven decided to "do his own thing." Lucifer tried to usurp the power and position of God and thus was thrown out of heaven. Satan has, for a brief period of time, limited power over the world —*but man always has the choice and means to resist his evil ways* (*see* Job and 1 Corinthians 10:13).

The last reason misfortune happens to us is *our personal sin and disobedience.* We as Christians are responsible for a lot more of our personal problems than we are often willing to admit. The Bible is filled with hundreds of examples of individuals or nations who have sinned and *as a result God has allowed them to suffer* at the hands of their enemies or friends, to lose possessions, home, job, family, or their own lives as a direct result of their personal sin. The person who has abused his or her body before or after accepting Christ will still suffer the normal consequences of that abuse. The person who smoked for twenty years and then accepts Christ and gives up smoking is still much more liable to get lung cancer than the person who never smoked. It's a fact that at least 50 percent of the problems, suffering, and illness that are evaluated by the average physician are psychosomatic, that is, they are induced by one's own mind. Unfortunately, I don't think the percentage is much less among Christians. Add to this diseases caused by abusing our bodies and I suspect that at least 70 percent of all illness and suffering is self-induced. *None of the situations in this category are the will of God* (*see* Joshua 7; 2 Kings 13:2, 3; 17:19, 20; 1 Chronicles 5:25, 26; 10:13; Judges 10:6–8; 1 Corinthians 11:18–31).

GOD WILL USE MISFORTUNES IN OUR LIVES FOR HIS AND OUR BENEFIT

Though God does not will your misfortune, He will utilize everything to His and our advantage if we will let Him.

Given your and my setting in life—no matter how good or bad —God makes available to us His perfect will for our lives. God uses suffering and misfortune to remind us that we are mortals, facing future judgment. Therefore, the first and most important purpose that adversity can serve is to initially bring us to a right relationship with God through accepting Christ as our personal Saviour.

The second way God uses affliction is to point out sin, when it is present, and to bring us back to Himself (*see* Joshua 7; 1 Corinthians 11:31, 32).

If sin is the cause of our suffering and if we are open, God will be specific and put His finger on the problem. Our responsibility is to admit the problem, accept His forgiveness, and begin walking in a way which is pleasing to God (*see* 1 John 1:9). However, *we should never conclude that because there is misfortune or adversity we have necessarily sinned.* If there is no sin, one should not indulge in morbid introspection or let Satan, the Accuser, or friends, for that matter, suggest that you have sinned (*see* Job 1:6 LB; Revelation 12:10). Many well-meaning but ill-informed Christians frequently do this, creating doubt, false guilt, and confusion in the lives of dear people who are already suffering (*see* the entire Book of Job).

We must be careful to see the purpose to which God wants to use suffering; not blaming someone else, even though another person may be partially responsible (*see* 1 Kings 18:17). When others are responsible for our suffering we must be willing to forgive:

> For if you forgive people their trespasses—that is their reckless and willful sins, leaving them, letting them go and giving up resentment—your heavenly Father will also forgive you. But if you do not forgive others their trespasses—their reckless and wilful sins, leaving them, letting them go and giving up resentment—neither will your Father forgive you your trespasses.
>
> Matthew 6:14, 15 AMPLIFIED.

This does not mean that you should minimize or justify their ill acts but it means that you are willing to forgive despite them. (For further details on dealing with responsibility, bitterness, and resentment *see Run and Not Be Weary* by the author.)

The third way God uses our misfortune is to teach, chasten, and build Christlike character. *It is my opinion that God is not the author or cause of the misfortune in our lives but that He uses the situations which we are confronted with in the daily experiences of living.* It's just like a loving parent; he doesn't have to cause or create any reasons for discipline—they are already there—what's necessary is to help the child mature and be responsible in the situations that naturally come his way (*see* Hebrews 5:8 LB; 12:9–11; James 1:2–5 LB; Romans 5:3–5 LB; 2 Corinthians 7:9–11; 12:7–10; 1 Peter 1:6, 7; Deuteronomy 8:2).

The fourth use to which He puts our adversity is to bring glory to His Name. Again, I don't believe He is the instigator of the difficulties but He will utilize them to the fullest if we will allow Him. Joseph's brothers were jealous of him but God protected Joseph from death though he suffered years of difficulty. I feel quite sure Joseph didn't understand during many of those years, nevertheless he remained faithful to God. When God raised him up to be second in command of all of Egypt this godly man's response to his brothers was: "As far as I am concerned, God turned into good what you meant for evil . . ." (Genesis 50:20 LB). The Bible is full of other examples of how God brought glory to His Name in adverse situations, such as healing the blind man and raising Lazarus from the grave (*see* John 9:1–15; 11:1–45).

CONCLUSION

God doesn't mind the sincere, honest question "Why did this misfortune happen to me?" In fact, that's the question He wants us to ask so that we will evaluate our lives and be sure we are following His will. But having done that we must be very careful that we don't linger at this point too long, for then we are probably becoming bitter and resistive individuals, blaming God or others. Job deliberately avoided accusing God, an example we should follow (*see* Job 1:21, 22; 38–41).

At times you may still be perplexed and you don't have to feel alone. Paul states in 2 Corinthians 4:8, "We are pressed on every side by troubles, but not crushed and broken. We are perplexed because we don't know why things happen as they do, but we don't give up and quit" (LB). Now we see through a "glass, darkly" but someday we will totally understand (*see* 1 Corinthians 13:12 KJV). His ways are higher than our ways and our minds just don't understand the mind-working of an infinite God (*see* Isaiah 55:8, 9). Periodically the proverb (20:24) must be applied which states: "Since the Lord is directing our steps, why try to understand everything that happens along the way?" (LB). In some Christian circles there is a tendency to "manufacture" some spiritual reason for everything that happens—this may be unwise. We don't have to explain to ourselves or to others why everything happens to us.

In the final analysis, our attitude toward difficulties has a much greater effect on us and others than the actual circumstances. Brother Lawrence (*The Practice of the Presence of God*), a monk in the seventeenth century said, "The sorest afflictions never appear intolerable except when we see them in the wrong light." God is more concerned about our response than the problem. The right attitude is often the first step to the solution. Our response to what happens may actually determine whether or not there is a solution. Job had to be willing to actually pray for his falsely accusing friends in order that they might come into a right relationship with God. As an incidental result, God restored Job's wealth and happiness! In fact, the Lord gave him twice as much as before (*see* Job 42:10).

We praise God in adverse situations, not necessarily because we feel like it, but because it's commended. We rejoice, not for the evil done, but that God will see us through it and ultimately triumph. We are told, "Always be joyful. . . . No matter what happens, always be thankful, for *this is God's will* for you who belong to Christ Jesus" (1 Thessalonians 5:16–18 LB author's italics).

We can be assured that God will help us in every difficult situation: "For God has said, 'I will never, *never* fail you nor forsake you.' That is why we can say without any doubt of fear, 'The Lord is my Helper and I am not afraid of anything that mere man can do to me' " (Hebrews 13:5, 6 LB; *see also* 1 Peter 4:12–19; Psalms 34:19; Psalms 112 LB).

With each problem we are assured that God will find a way to use it to His glory and our good. He promises: "And we know that all that happens to us is working for our good if we love God and are fitting into his plans" (Romans 8:28 LB).

QUESTIONS

1.   I recently read this statement. "The world should see a Christian as the Word sees him; a man able to control his circumstances with every physical, mental and spiritual need met." What do you think of this statement?

2.   Is it wise to always find a reason for misfortune? How hard should we look for a reason? Why do some people "manufacture" reasons?

3.   My brother was a medical missionary killed by Congolese rebels at thirty-eight years of age. I can think of at least four possible reasons why this might have occurred. How many can you list? What is the difference between this question and "manufacturing" reasons for a tragedy?

4.   It is often stated that God has a plan for our lives. How does that fit in with adversity and misfortune?

5.   Yesterday I attended the funeral of a good friend who had for many years been a devoted follower of Christ. She suffered and died in middle age, leaving behind a young family that needed her. Another friend said to me at the funeral, "It's good to know that God makes no mistakes—that all of these things happen according to His plan." How would you respond to such a statement? Do you think God was the prime mover in this event?

PART TWO

PREREQUISITES FOR KNOWING GOD'S WILL

Therefore, my brothers, I implore you by God's mercy to offer your very selves to him: a living sacrifice. . . . Adapt yourselves no longer to the pattern of this present world, but let your minds be remade and your whole nature thus transformed. *Then you will be able to discern the will of God*, and to know what is good, acceptable, and perfect. (Romans 12:1–3 NEB author's italics)

Undoubtedly the single most important element necessary if we would know God's will is a life yielded and obedient to Christ. In this section I have elaborated on what this means. Also, certain other prerequisites are discussed in order to place us in a better position to determine His will in a given matter. This section is really the crux of *living* God's will.

14
GOD'S WILL: AN ALL-CONSUMING DESIRE

Knowing God, pleasing God, and doing His will cannot be a secondary concern or a casual pursuit. If we would know God and His will it must be of prime importance to us. In fact, knowing God and pleasing Him should be the most important thing in our lives, an all-consuming desire. The rich young ruler found out that just one thing standing in the way was sufficient to keep Him from God and His will. You cannot expect God to lead you in one area of your life unless you are willing to be led in all areas. You cannot expect Him to guide you at all unless you are willing to let Him guide you in all.

A.W. Tozer says in *The Divine Conquest,* "To will the will of God is to do more than give unprotesting consent to it; it is rather to choose God's will with positive determination . . . that is just what he most ardently desires."

Paul says:

> But all these things that I once thought very worthwhile—now I've thrown them all away so that I can put my trust and hope in Christ alone. Yes, everything else is worthless when compared with the priceless gain of knowing Christ Jesus my Lord. I have put aside all else, counting it worth less than nothing, in order that I can have Christ. . . . Now I have given up everything else—I have found it to be the only way to really know Christ. . . .
>
> Philippians 3:7–10 LB

Isn't this really what the first commandment is all about: "You shall love the Lord your God with all your heart, and with all your soul, and with all your mind, and with all your strength" (Mark 12:30).

Again, I would emphasize that seeking God's will must be the central aim of our life. The person who is unwilling to pursue God will never really know God's will. However, I want to inject a word of caution to the sensitive person. The more reflective, possibly introverted person may be overly critical of himself. He can always find some area of his life where he could have done better, worked harder, given of himself more, sought God's will more diligently.

Though I believe we must put God first in our life, seeking His will above everything else, at the same time we must rest in Him. Hebrews 4 emphasizes the importance of learning to enter into God's rest. Once we have put God first, have dealt with any known sin, and are in fellowship with Him through His Word and prayer, we can rest in His will (*see* chapters 21 through 25). We must always be open to any new leading. But we must also learn —especially those of us who are very sensitive—to cease being uptight about pushing ourselves to know and do more. We can be assured that God will take over and help us as Paul says He will: "For God is at work within you, helping you want to obey him, and then helping you do what he wants" (Philippians 2:13 LB).

QUESTIONS

*1. To what extent do you want God's will:
   (a) not at all
   (b) a little
   (c) moderately
   (d) quite a bit
   (e) I want to want the will of God in my life
   (f) more than anything else in the world

*2.   Why don't you want more of God and His will:
        (a) because of frank sin
        (b) misconceptions about the Christian life
        (c) unwilling to step out
        (d) afraid it will cost us too much
        (e) other [specify]

3.   Would you classify yourself as one who:
        (a) needs to give God's will more consideration
        (b) has a proper understanding of and obedience to God's will
        (c) is hypersensitive and tends to be unduly critical of your-
            self, your motives, your desires, and efforts. (If the latter
            is the case, why are you so critical? Are there some under-
            lying reasons you have not faced?)

15
GOD'S WILL IS PRIMARILY "TO BE"

For decades Satan has effectively deceived many sincere,
dedicated Christians into believing that God's will is primarily
related to profession or geographical location. Thus they become concerned about a "call" to the mission field or ministry, whether or not to be a physician, lawyer, or businessman.
They then worry about *where* they should serve the Lord—if
in the city, which city; and if in an underdeveloped country,
which one. Their anxiety about being in God's will includes
whether or not they should serve on a given committee, teach
a certain Sunday-school class, or get involved in other worth-
while programs.

If I seek only the answers to my questions of direction, I will get no answers. But if I seek God first, the directions I need will be given. So often we want a blueprint for the next twenty-five years and God doesn't give out blueprints. He gives us the Guide, the Planner, the Maker of blueprints, His Son, Christ, as revealed to us primarily through God's Word and the Holy Spirit, so that we will be dependent on Him.

John 6:29 says, "This is the will of God, that you believe in the one he has sent" (LB). Focusing more on the plan than the Planner is idolatry, and many of us are guilty of such idolatry. Mary, you recall, learned to worship Christ, while her sister, Martha, anxiously worked for Him.

Frequently God reveals His will to us after we worship Him without any thought of what He wants us to do—without any work, program, plan, or striving to know His will. Acts 13:2 says, "One day as these men were worshiping and fasting the Holy Spirit said, 'Dedicate Barnabas and Paul for a special job I have for them' " (LB). They weren't seeking the will of God, they were worshiping God and in the process were led to the specific task He had for them.

Remember Philip, who was living God's will. When God wanted him in a different location God took the responsibility to clearly reveal that to him (*see* Acts 8). On the other hand, there was Jonah, who was sometimes in the wrong location, sometimes in the right location, but in the recorded Scriptures he never really lived in God's will.

God's will, then, has more to do with our spiritual condition than our geographical location. It is not tied up in the profession but in the kind of person I am. If I am the right kind of person, God will quickly alter the other details if they are important to Him. After all, I can be in the right place and perform the right duties, but if I am not the right kind of person, all my effort is wood, hay, and stubble in God's eyes (*see* 1 Corinthians 3:11–15). I might even marry the right individual, but if I do not continue becoming the right person, I will not be in God's will.

This brings me to the next point. Often the Christian tends to orient his entire life around "doing"—accomplishing thus and so for God when God's program is primarily "to be"—being the person He wants me to be. We tend to frantically run to meetings, engage in many charitable works, and do good things for God. We read in 1 Thessalonians 4:3, "For this is the will of God, your sanctification . . ." which means that our lives are consecrated for sacred use; they are pure. Romans 12:1 and 2 indicates not only that God wants us to be assured of our salvation but also that we should be completely dedicated, separated, and transformed individuals. The Scriptures go even further by saying, "You shall be holy, for I am holy" (1 Peter 1:16; *see also* Leviticus 20:7).

God's will, then, is a way of life. It means first of all that we have accepted Christ as our Saviour and that there is no known sin in our life (*see* 1 Timothy 2:4; Psalms 66:18). We must be feeding on His Word faithfully if we are to grow in our spiritual life and be healthy Christians (*see* 1 Peter 2:2, 3). A prayer life and fellowship with other Christians are of vital importance (*see* Hebrews 10:25). More will be said about these specific topics in part 3.

Another way in which the Christian is deceived is by being more concerned about the future than the *now*. The highest will of God is that in whatever circumstances I find myself, I am doing what pleases Him—*now*. The past is gone, though we certainly can learn from it; but beyond that we can do virtually nothing about it. The future is not yet, though we may have a distant outline of what God has for us later. Some plans and preparations are necessary for the future, but we have to be exceedingly careful that we aren't wasting time living in the future (*see* chapters 18, 19, 20; Matthew 6:34; Hebrews 3:7–15).

For the most part God wants us to live in the now. He has only given us the now, and His prime concern is "now obedience." That is, am I doing His will, right now? Am I allowing Him to guide me, right now? Am I in fellowship with Him, free of unconfessed sin, and available for anything He wants me to do, right now? (*See* Matthew 8:22 LB.)

If you are confused about the future or possibly the past, the place to start is to do His will *now*. That may be as seemingly a minute thing as the studies that are waiting, some household responsibility, or an attitude to be dealt with. It has been amazing to me how many times when I have been confused or wondered about His will—when I have paused and asked, "What is the one thing that You want me to do now?"—the answer has been loud and clear. Doing the one thing He directs has erased the confusion and given peace. Then one finds that as he is obedient in the little daily events of life, His will unfolds. Exodus 16:4 explains how God planned to feed the children of Israel on a day-by-day basis. They were to go out each day and gather just enough food for that day. And God said, "I will test them in this, to see whether they will follow my instructions or not" (LB).

We need to decide to do what God has revealed for this day. We must not allow ourselves to be anxious about the future. We will follow Him step by step, day by day, being obedient in the now, trusting Him for the future. A good life resolve might be: I will always do God's will so far as I know it.

QUESTIONS

*1. To what extent do you become more enamored with the plan than the Planner?

2. Why is it idolatry to be more interested in God's will than in Christ Himself?

3. What is misleading about the questions "Should I marry Jane or Sue?" and "Should I be a full-timer or layman?"

4. Can a person marry the right person and have the wrong marriage? Explain.

*5. Do you find you mainly think about the future when you consider God's will? Why?

6. To what extent do we need to plan for the future?

7. Why do you think we want "to do" instead of "to be"? Is this just a play on words?

8.   Often we ask ourselves, "Am I doing the will of God?" or "What is the will of God for me?" Should this be changed to *"Am* I the will of God?"

9.   Is the term *holiness* outdated for this age? What does it mean and what does it not mean? Give a good synonym. *Is your life holy?

10.   Are you now the kind of a person God wants you to be? If you are not, is there any use in further seeking God's will?

11.   Does the application of "now obedience" really work? Give an example from your own life.

16
REQUIRED: CONFIDENCE THAT HE WILL LEAD YOU

If you want to know what God wants you to do, ask him, and he will gladly tell you, for he is always ready to give a bountiful supply of wisdom to all who ask him; he will not resent it. But when you ask him, *be sure that you really expect him to tell you,* for a doubtful mind will be as unsettled as a wave of the sea that is driven and tossed by the wind; and every decision you then make will be uncertain, as you turn first this way, and then that. If you don't ask with faith, don't expect the Lord to give you any solid answer.

James 1:5–8 LB author's italics

What is faith? It is the confident assurance that something we want is going to happen. It is the certainty that what we hope for is waiting for us, even though we cannot see it up ahead. Men of God in days of old were famous for their faith. . . . You can never please God without faith, without depending on him. Anyone who wants to come to God must believe that there is a God and that he rewards those who sincerely look for him.

Hebrews 11:1, 2, 6 LB

Throughout the entire eleventh chapter of Hebrews, and other Scriptures, we find that a prerequisite for being led by God is the utmost confidence and trust in God Himself. This is crucial before we even think about His leading us. In addition to this we must have confidence that He will, in fact, lead us. This may include times when we don't know where we are being led such as happened to Abraham (*see* Hebrews 11:8). A.W. Tozer tells us in *The Knowledge of the Holy,* "We shall not seek to understand in order that we may believe but to believe in order that we may understand." God will at times require that we step out in faith —before we really understand where, how, or why He is leading us in such a way.

"Oh, what a wonderful God we have! How great are his wisdom and knowledge and riches! How impossible it is for us to understand his decisions and his methods!" (Romans 11:33 LB). Our faith in God and the assurance that He will lead us will help us through those times when we don't understand His methods in our lives.

QUESTIONS

1. Why is it important to realize that we must trust Him to lead us?
2. If you don't have faith, how can you get it?
3. Should our faith be blind? Explain your answer.
4. What is the place of our responsibility in arriving at a decision? Are faith and our efforts in knowing God's will mutually exclusive?

17
NEEDED: A PROPER INDEPENDENCE

When all kinds of trials . . . crowd into your lives . . . welcome them as friends! . . . and you will find you have *become men of mature character with the right sort of independence.* And if in the process, any of you does not know how to meet any particular problem, he has only to ask God—who gives generously. . . .

James 1:2–5 PHILLIPS, italics author's

A prerequisite for knowing God's will is "the right sort of independence." Dependence upon God necessitates a certain independence of people and possessions. This independence involves not only the obvious sinful things such as lust, worldly things, or an abnormal attachment to riches (*see* 1 John 2:15–17) but also the more difficult independence which is in our relationships with other people. You see, to be dependent upon God necessitates a certain amount of independence even toward other Christians. A.T. Pierson says of George Müller in *George Müller of Bristol*, ". . . His resolve was unbroken to follow the Lord's leading at any cost, but he now clearly saw that he could be *independent of man only by being more entirely dependent on God.* . . ."

This independence doesn't mean we become indifferent to others or their needs, nor does it mean becoming irresponsible or unreliable. We can still work in close proximity with others and under God's concurrence, even receive direction from other Christians. It certainly does not mean we can't have a close, loving relationship with others. What it does mean is that *all* relationships are subservient to our relationship with Jesus Christ (*see* Luke 14:26).

The Scriptures are full of examples of the proper kind of independence toward others. In fact, virtually every person in the Scriptures whom God used is an example of this independence. Certainly the Old Testament prophets are a key example, as well as the New Testament disciples. Even Paul retained a certain independence from the other disciples. So often when God directs us some well-meaning individual who does not understand God's leading in our life tries "for our good" to show us God's will. Peter was guilty of this with his Lord. Christ's response to Peter's well-intended advice was, "Get behind me, Satan! You are a hindrance to me . . ." (Matthew 16:23). Numerous godly men in the decades since have had to wrestle with this same problem of being misunderstood by people due to their obedience to God. Martin Luther and George Müller are only the start of a long list.

Hannah Whitall Smith says in *The Christian's Secret of a Happy Life:*

> . . . You must therefore realize that His very love for you may perhaps lead you to run counter to the loving wishes of even your dearest friends. You must learn, from Luke 14:26–33, and similar passages, that in order to be a disciple and follower of your Lord, you may perhaps be called upon to forsake inwardly all that you have. . . . Unless the possibility of this is clearly recognized you will be very likely to get into difficulty, because it often happens that the child of God who enters upon this life of obedience is sooner or later led into paths which meet with the disapproval of those he best loves. . . .

I am currently evaluating the roll of a proper independence in my life. I am a physician who practices the specialty of internal medicine. I believe God has directed me to such a practice with a group in Southern California. When I joined the group of approximately twenty-five other physicians some six and one-half years ago, it seemed clear to me that this was God's will. So far as I knew I was joining them for the rest of my working lifetime. Yet, I had a strange feeling that I could not get my roots too deep, and an awareness that I must continue to remain open to any change in God's plan for my life. Recently God has led me to terminate this practice and take some specialty training in another field. As I contemplate making this change, I dread, from a human perspective, giving up the practice of internal medicine which I enjoy very much, giving up the relationship with the other doctors, and most important, the relationship with my patients. Emotionally, I find this very difficult. Many patients are close personal friends. Some have come to know Christ through my sharing the Gospel with them. If I were to dwell on this aspect much, or if I were to talk it over with them first, I am afraid I would never make the decision that I believe God would have me make. Instead I have spent numerous hours in prayer, consideration, fact-finding, and discussion, most of it alone but some of it with my wife. The decision was made away from any "people pressure."

The decision now has been made, the contract has been signed, and several months from now I will inform my patients in plenty of time for them to find another physician. Yes, that will be difficult, but I have learned from past experience that God will give grace when needed. But the point I am trying to make is that this decision had to be made behind closed doors while seeking God's will. Now I must carry out that decision regardless of the difficulty. I must have "the right sort of independence."

QUESTIONS

1. Why is a chapter like this needed—don't most people err on being too independent?
2. Define the qualities in "the right sort of independence."
3. Define the characteristics in the wrong sort of independence.
4. List three examples from God's Word of a person exercising the right sort of independence.

18
GOD'S LEADING REQUIRES PERSONAL RESPONSIBILITY

An obese patient had just gotten off the scales and again had not lost any weight. She is a fine, very active, sincere Christian woman who had several medical problems that made it doubly important she lose weight. I had been stressing this for a number of weeks but apparently to no avail. So I kindly but firmly said, "You know, you really must work on this. It's crucial for your health." To which she commented, *"The Lord willing,* next time I will lose weight."

"What do you mean, 'The Lord willing'?" I blurted out, somewhat surprising myself. "He's willing. The question is—are you?"

Then there was the night I was leading a home Bible study. We were discussing our responsibility in matters. One well-meaning woman's emphatic comment was, "Just let God direct; have no will of your own and you will know His will." Our host, who was a young Christian, turned to her and asked, "You know those oatmeal cookies you brought tonight—whose responsibility was it that the oatmeal was left out—God, Satan, or you?"

So often we Christians use God and "God's will" as an excuse when we fail in our responsibilities. We look for an easy road to achieve anything and everything—an easy road to learning, an easy road to working, an easy road to thinking, planning, deciding. Clichés like "The Lord led me" or "Trust" or "Only have faith" often become nothing more than "superspiritual" excuses. Even in early Christendom we find this. The Christians of Thessalonica were rebuked by Paul for stopping their work and waiting for God's return. *Total commitment to Christ is never a substitute for thinking or action.* In fact, you cannot remain a committed

Christian without thinking and exercising appropriate responsible action.

Recently a lady came to me with recurring abdominal pain and other symptoms. I had seen her several times, we had done a number of tests, and still her symptoms did not fit the usual disease processes. One evening I saw her on an emergency basis and her husband, who is a dedicated Christian, said to me, "It must be a lot easier as a Christian, facing problems like this." I asked him what he meant. Did he mean it was easier to take care of Christians who are sick, or that diagnosing and treating illness was easier as a Christian physician than it would be for a non-Christian? He indicated he meant the latter. I was a little perplexed by this question, but as honestly as I could I said no. His wife had all of our usual tests. I felt fairly sure of the diagnosis, but before finally recommending major surgery, I had another physician see her to verify our impression and recommendations.

But the question posed by the woman's husband came back to me many times. I asked myself, Am I lacking in my relationship or yieldedness to God, so that He can't reveal things to me that would make a diagnosis and treatment easier? Should I, as a Christian physician, be able to diagnose an illness faster than a non-Christian doctor? It would be nice for both the patient and myself if many of the tests could be avoided. The fact of the matter is, of course, that God expects me as a Christian physician to go through the same steps as a non-Christian. I certainly should ask God to direct me and I should look for His guidance, but I cannot take any shortcuts. Certainly God may choose to supersede all of these usual steps—but I believe that is the exception to the rule.

There is a great tendency in Christianity to migrate to extremes on the matter of personal responsibility versus faith and trust. Let me illustrate with two groups I call the "superspiritual" and the "cool and logical."

First, the "superspiritual," who might more appropriately be called the "pseudosuperspiritual." These sincere Christians overemphasize "Just trust God." They will often say, "It is great to go out on a limb—and see God work." They imply that if you don't leave everything to God, you aren't really trusting Him. The "pseudosuperspiritual" disregards wisdom, judgment, and common sense. He emphasizes such verses as "Trust in the Lord with all thine heart; and lean not unto thine own understanding," "For the wisdom of this world is foolishness with God," and "I will destroy the wisdom of the wise" (Proverbs 3:5 KJV; 1 Corinthians 3:19 KJV; 1:19). However, verses like these used out of context often result in bad decisions, disillusionment, bitterness, and resentment by people who make some unwise decisions in Christ's Name. It leads to dishonesty and putting on the mask, if not open rejection of God.

The opposite of the "superspiritual" is the "cool and logical" Christian. He has overreacted to his pseudospiritual brother, and emphasizes, "Use your head, God gave it to you. Don't do anything rash." He may even say, "God helps those who help themselves." Before long he has taken anything that is supernatural away from God and the Christian's relationship with God. He has lost sight of the appropriate and essential place of faith and trust. The Pharisees did this. They were so cool and logical they froze Christ right out of their lives. God and the working of the Holy Spirit is void in the lives of "cool and logical" Christians. Legalism inevitably creeps in. If they are capable individuals they become self-sufficient and rely on their own human efforts. If they are not so capable they become depressed and dejected. There are valid scriptural principles on both sides. But if either view is carried to the extreme the truth becomes distorted and havoc is the result.

Certainly we must emphasize the place of faith. We come to Christ and receive His salvation only through faith. Our works can add absolutely nothing to His completed work. Likewise our walk in Christ is by faith. All of my efforts, all of my responsible actions amount to a hill of beans when compared to God's absolute standard of perfection and holiness. In the matter of knowing God's will it is essential to have faith in God and the fact that He will guide us. But this faith never negates the appropriate place of our full responsibility. The Scriptures clearly teach personal responsibility in a number of areas; included are a willingness to work, to obtain knowledge and wisdom, and to use appropriate discernment and judgment.

The oft-quoted Proverbs 3:5, 6 says, "Trust in the Lord with all thine heart; *and lean not unto thine own understanding.* In all thy ways acknowledge him, and he shall direct thy paths" (KJV author's italics). It says not to *lean* or *rely* on your own understanding; it doesn't say not to *use* your understanding.

What conclusions and personal applications can we now make? First of all, we should actively seek to be responsible and wise Christians. This is enlightened wisdom that utilizes all the natural abilities and resources God has given us. It is enlightened by God's Word and the eternal outlook, perspective, and value system. It is tempered and directed by the Holy Spirit.

Second, we should never be afraid to utilize proven benefits of the world when they are not in conflict with the Scriptures or God's directed will for us.

Third, we must be willing to do all the work, whether physical or mental, that a non-Christian must do to arrive at the same point, goal, occupation, or result. Our effort not only helps in most situations but God also, in fact, expects it of us. For example, if I am going to buy a car, it would be nice if God would just direct me to the right party and put His finger on the car that I should buy. It would save a lot of work. However, usually I find I must do the research, inquire, examine cars, review *Consumer Reports,* and use the best judgment I can, all the while seeking God's direction in the matter. Proverbs 16:9 says, "We should make plans—counting on God to direct us" (LB).

Dr. David A. Seamands aptly speaks to this point in his tape "Principles for Choosing a Mate" (from a series on Christian Marriage and Home, available through Tape Ministers, Box

3389, Pasadena, CA 91103). He says, "God does not choose your mate for you. The choosing of a life's partner is a decision, which in the final analysis, is your decision. It's your choice; and the responsibility for it . . . rests squarely on your shoulders. . . . That's not to say God doesn't guide us in our decision."

Fourth, along with doing our part we must be willing to commit anything and everything we have done to God. Sometimes the supernatural will intervene in ways which are His ways and above our ways. We can't understand them. Occasionally God may violate some natural law such as when Peter walked on the water or when Abraham had to be willing to sacrifice his own son. Many times after we have used all our resources, we realize that this is a matter in which we are totally incapable.

Fifth, we must realize we are flesh and blood. All of our capabilities, all of our wisdom, insights, and work are totally a gift from God. We are truly unprofitable servants doing just what is expected of us (*see* Luke 17:10). In the final analysis we can never rely on our own insight or abilities (*see* Proverbs 3:5). It is never the big "I." It is never trusting in man so that it in any way excludes God. The attitude depicted in Isaiah 10:13, "By the strength of *my hand I have done it,* and by *my wisdom,* for *I have understanding* . . ." (author's italics) is always an abomination to God.

So, to summarize: I believe the Scriptures teach the Christian a beautiful and proper balance of both trust and responsibility, faith and works. This is one of the tremendous paradoxes in the Word and one which is often poorly understood. While we are exercising our faith in God, He has given us the responsibility to develop and use our intellect, human capabilities, and judgment. The Christian's work is neither intellect without faith nor faith without intellect. There may be times when we walk by faith, despite intellect, but one must never rely on intellect. God takes over when our intellect becomes inadequate; however, God's wisdom is never contradictory to the Spirit-controlled and enlightened intellect.

QUESTIONS

1. It has been said, "Pray as if it all depends upon God, work as if everything depends upon you, plan as if it depends on both of us." What do you think of this philosophy?

2. Proverbs 3:4, 5 says, "If you want favor with both God and man, and a reputation for good judgment and common sense, then trust the Lord completely; don't ever trust yourself" (LB). What does it mean to never trust yourself?

3. The Apostle Paul lived by faith. He felt called to the ministry and for the most part was considered a full-timer. However, on one occasion he ran short of money and took a secular occupation. Do you think this would have happened if he had had "more faith"?

4. Is the person who "just trusts God" irresponsible?

5. One Sunday I heard a well-known minister preach that "Christ can meet every need you have—you are complete in Him." There was no qualification to this often-heard statement. What is really meant by such a statement? How does this fit with the Scriptures and lives of dedicated Christians you know? Does this mean that Christ, without any other human involvement, will meet your needs for food, health, education, and transportation? Please clarify.

19
GOD'S WILL REQUIRES INITIATIVE

Tonight while driving home from work I was thinking how fortunate I am to have such a wonderful wife and two great children. I mused how I might show them my love. I could bring home some roses, but the ones my wife grows are as beautiful as the florists'. Last month I brought her some perfume. It has been a long time since I have brought her a nice box of candy and I'm sure the kids would enjoy some. So I bought a box for Betty and two smaller ones for Greg and Susan.

I could have called home first and said, "Honey, what is your will tonight—what would you like me to bring home?"

She might have replied, "A half-gallon of milk and a loaf of bread." Not quite what I had in mind. I might have explained that I wanted to bring her something special to let her know of my appreciation for her and the children. I am sure she would have replied, "I know that." Yet I know she appreciates it if I take a little extra time and thought to reassure her of my love. When you love someone you are willing to exert yourself and take the initiative in a loving way.

We find examples of initiative in the Scriptures. For instance, take the situation of David and three of his men. David was hiding from the Philistines and he longed for some tasty water from the well of Bethlehem. He casually mentioned this to a few of his men. There was no command that they should get some water, just the expression of a deep, inward longing. But to the three men, the saying "Your wish is my command" became in essence a reality. These men, unbeknown to anyone, including David, went through enemy lines risking their lives to obtain water for David, their king. This act of love was "beyond the call of duty." And though David did not feel as though he could drink this water because it represented the lives of his men, he eventually promoted them to top positions (*see* 1 Chronicles 11:15–19).

Perhaps you are thinking that it is really God who takes the initiative in our lives. It is true that a man cannot come to Christ unless God draws him (*see* John 6:44). John 16:8 also says that the Holy Spirit "will convince the world of its sin, and of the availability of God's goodness, and of deliverance from judgment" (LB). So the Holy Spirit's work is to deal with our hearts in a way which points us to Christ. We must decide whether or not we will respond to His "still small voice" (1 Kings 19:12) which is prodding us to come to grips with our relationship with God. After we receive Christ, obvious sins such as lying, cheating, illicit sex, and the like will be brought to our attention by the Holy Spirit as being sinful and out of God's will. Hopefully, other Christians will show us that to grow in the Christian life we must be continually exposed to God's Word, the Bible, and be involved in meaningful Christian fellowship.

But as we start to grow *our initiative* becomes of greater and greater importance as we put on the whole armor of God and manifest the fruit of the spirit, etc. (*See* Ephesians 6:10–18; Galatians 5:16–24.) There will be many times when God will not directly prod us any further, but will allow us the opportunity to use our initiative to fulfill those things which are clearly upon His heart as revealed in His Word. This may well be what Paul means in Philippians 2:12, 13 when he speaks about working out what God has given us, remembering always that God is at work in us.

I believe the Scriptures teach that those who pleased the Lord the most were not just obedient when they received a personal specific command. They were also men who knew what pleased God and took the initiative in fulfilling those things that pleased Him. Remember the example of Solomon in Chapter 9.

Another example is when Moses interceded in behalf of the children of Israel so that God would not hurt His own Name (*see* Exodus 32:7–14). Abraham interceded for others by praying for the righteous in Sodom and Gomorrah (*see* Genesis 18:20–19:29). Isaiah was close enough to God to hear His concern, "Whom shall I send, and who will go for us?" Isaiah, taking the initiative, replied, "Here am I! Send me" (Isaiah 6:8).

As we have already seen, the Apostle Paul "took the bull by the horns" in initiating those things which were obviously on God's heart—preaching the Gospel and building up Christians. Only as Paul and Barnabas went forth did the Holy Spirit intervene and direct in the specific areas He wanted them to go. I doubt if the Holy Spirit would have directed them in the sixteenth chapter of Acts had they not taken the initiative in the fifteenth. Paul's missionary journeys are very revealing along this line. In 2 Corinthians 2:12, for example, only when he came to the town of Troas to preach the Gospel was a door opened for him.

This is also the emphasis of the parable of the talents (*see* Matthew 25; Luke 19). The nobleman, representing Christ, left his servants with resources to invest while he was in a distant country. It appears that the entire initiative of investing was left up to the servants. When the nobleman returned, he considered those faithful who invested and reaped an increase. The one servant who was afraid to invest—but kept his gift intact, unused, and took no risks, was considered a wicked servant. He was further chided by the nobleman for not at least depositing his talent in the bank and getting some return.

In the business world a man who has resources and initiative can reap a tenfold profit. Yes, it requires physical and mental work and risk. If the man has money and is unwilling to take the initiative or the risk for higher gains, then he should at least deposit it in a bank where it will be invested for him, providing a smaller but predictable profit.

Every Christian has been given a certain talent or gift and if he is unwilling, afraid, or unable (?) to take the initiative in investing it in God's kingdom, he should link up with other yielded Christians organized to lead him in doing those things on God's heart. In this way he will be able to reap some reward from his investment and in the process please his Lord. I am afraid I see no excuse for the person who doesn't know what to do for God or His kingdom. There are so many opportunities if one is willing to take a little initiative.

"There is none that . . . stirreth up himself to take hold of thee . . ." lamented the Prophet Isaiah (64:7 KJV). Proverbs 16:9 says, "We should make plans" (LB). I believe this means we should take the initiative but always "counting on God to direct us" (LB). This is what 1 Corinthians 12:31 means when it says, "The higher gifts are those you should aim at" (NEB).

Here again a quote from A.W. Tozer is appropriate. He states in *The Divine Conquest:*

To will the will of God is to do more than give unprotesting consent to it; it is rather to choose God's will with positive determination. As the work of God advances the Christian finds himself free to choose whatever he will and he gladly chooses the will of God as his highest conceivable good. Such a man has found life's highest goal. He has been placed beyond the little disappointments that plague the rest of men. Whatever happens to him is the will of God for him, and that is just what he most ardently desires. But it is only fair to state that this condition is one not reached by many of the busy Christians of our busy times. Until it is reached however, the Christian's peace cannot be complete. . . .

QUESTIONS

1. Do you really believe God expects personal initiative beyond what He directly reveals to you? Have you undertaken some spiritual activity due to personal initiative? What was it? How did it work out?

2. Do you think the issue of personal initiative could be overemphasized, especially to a very sensitive person? What might be the results of that?

3. Do you think God ever condones idle Christians? What is the place of rest and relaxation? (*Consider* Mark 6:30–32; Hebrews 4, etc.)

4. In your opinion, what is the proper application of the parable of the talents? Is it really stressing personal initiative?

5. Should we ever take personal initiative to do something for God when He has already told us what to do? (*See* 1 Samuel 13:8–13; 15:18–22; 2 Kings 20:1–6.) Can you think of any other examples? How does this fit with the parable of the widow who was commended for pleading with the judge? (*See* Luke 18:1–8.)

6. What are the higher gifts for which we should aim? List. How do you reconcile aiming for, or as the King James Version puts it, to "covet earnestly the best gifts" (1 Corinthians 12:31)? Is a gift something you seek?

20
HAVE A GAME PLAN

If I hadn't had a game plan, I probably would have married the wrong girl. Being a typical fellow, I was interested in girls and did my share of dating. At two particular times in my life there were two girls in whom I was especially interested. In fact, I was quite serious about both of them. They were both Christians since I believed that a Christian should not date a non-Christian (*see* 2 Corinthians 6:14). They went to church and were somewhat active in Christian activities. But I felt a little uneasy about both relationships. Though they would gladly talk about spiritual things when the subject was initiated, there didn't seem to be the deep, spontaneous interest that I knew was important.

Fortunately, I had seen some bad marriages and knew that the person I married would have a gigantic effect on all areas of my life, especially the spiritual aspect. Because of this I got alone with God, with my Bible, and some paper, and prayerfully thought through this area of my life. On a prayer page I wrote, "If You (God) have a girl for me, may You provide the following things in her life so that my ministry may be increased and in no way hindered. May she: 1. Put You first (in her life)." My list included some twenty items. Eleventh on the list was that she might be attractive—not that appearance wasn't important to me, but I had observed that with so many fellows beauty was number one on their unwritten list, and too often nothing else was very important. I put my list on a prayer page to be remembered each Sunday. It not only served to remind me to pray about this important aspect of my life each week but it also kept these standards indelibly printed on my mind—probably the reason I didn't marry the wrong girl.

Waiting until I was twenty-seven years of age was sometimes hard, but how thankful I am to God for the wonderful person He ultimately allowed me to marry. And incidentally, she does a great job of meeting the criteria on my list. I must admit that a few of the items on that list which I composed in 1954 are now rather amusing. But the point is that it served a tremendous purpose in my life for which I am grateful.

During the same period of my life, while in the navy I was challenged by another Christian fellow to consider my purpose and goal in life. Essential to this was the "game plan"—the means, strategy, intermediate steps or goals required to obtain the ultimate goal. This I found highly provocative and it has probably affected every area of my life since. I used Colossians 1:28, 29 (PHILLIPS) as a basis. My purpose or goal in life was to glorify God through a faithful, victorious, Christ-centered, Spirit-filled life, and to be fruitful by leading men to a saving knowledge of Christ, and to teach them all I had learned about following Christ so that they, in turn, could do likewise.

After this I listed my intermediate goals and then short-range goals. These were stepping-stones to my ultimate goal. Some of the intermediate goals I have necessarily changed as God's leading has been dynamic. In fact, I am not at all sure I would list my ultimate goal quite the same way if I were doing that assignment today. Nevertheless, the prayerful consideration of the Scriptures and God's will for my life helped me formulate a game plan. This has been indispensable in giving me purpose and direction. I believe it has helped me to be within God's perfect will for my life more of the time than I would have been without a game plan.

There are many examples in the Bible of individuals with clear-cut plans and goals—game plans, if you will. When He was twelve years of age, Christ asked His parents, ". . . wist ye not that I must be about my Father's business?" (Luke 2:49 KJV). At this early age, His purpose in life was clearly being manifest. We later find that He trained twelve men so that they would be able to share His message with the world (*see* John 17). It is of interest to note that, while in His body of flesh and blood, Christ had some internal struggles like the rest of us. We read that He was "deeply troubled." But we find His course so well established that though He reasoned to Himself, "Shall I pray, 'Father, save me from what lies ahead'?" He quickly responded to His own question by saying, "But that is the very reason why I came!" (John 12:27 LB). It seems even Christ had to struggle with the weakness of the flesh. But having a "game plan" helped clarify His objectives and gave Him added impetus to be obedient during perhaps the most vulnerable moment in His life.

Nehemiah had a game plan which helped him rebuild the walls of Jerusalem. In the New Testament Paul had a clear-cut game plan. Philippians 3:14 says, "I go straight for the goal—my reward the honor of my high calling by God in Christ Jesus" (PHILLIPS). In 1 Corinthians 9:24–26 LB he says:

> In a race, everyone runs but only one person gets first prize. So run your race to win. To win the contest you must deny yourselves many things that would keep you from doing your best. An athlete goes to all this trouble just to win a blue ribbon or a silver cup, but we do it for a heavenly reward that never disappears. So *I run straight to the goal with purpose in every step.* I fight to win, I'm not just shadowboxing or playing around.
>
> author's italics

Colossians 1:28, 29 clarifies Paul's goal even further: "So, naturally, we proclaim Christ! We warn everyone we meet, and we teach everyone we can, all that we know about him, so that, if possible, we may bring every man up to his full maturity in Christ Jesus. This is what I am working at all the time, with all the strength that God gives me" (PHILLIPS).

God has a plan for you and me. In 2 Timothy 1:9 we read, "Who hath saved us, and called us with an holy calling, not according to our works, but according to his own purpose and grace, which was given us in Christ Jesus before the world began" (KJV).

There are many things that a game plan will do for you. It will help you get your eyes off yourself. It will help you forget the past, whether good or bad (*see* Philippians 3:13). It will help you have a vision (*see* Proverbs 29:18 KJV). It will help you travel in a straight line to a set objective, therefore helping you become more efficient (*see* Proverbs 3:5, 6). Plans help make discipline more understandable and bearable. We are reminded in Matthew 26:41 that "the spirit indeed is willing, but the flesh is weak." A game plan helps us overcome the weakness of the flesh and decreases discouragement (*see* John 12:27 and Hebrews 12:1–3). It will encourage you to think ahead and weigh the long-term consequences of the course of action you are contemplating (*see* Deuteronomy 32:29; Luke 14:28–32). With an overall plan you will view individual decisions from a different perspective than the individual who skips helter-skelter through life.

A man who aims at nothing will hit it every time. A ship without a compass or destination will invariably become shipwrecked. So many people live such fragmented lives, the victims of the pressures of the many good things they really *should* do. The man with a purpose, however, is motivated by the things he *must* do. Christ said, "I *must* be about my Father's business." The person with a game plan doesn't have the time for very many *shoulds.*

If you don't have a game plan, you probably will have a plan —a plan to fail. If someone knew your thoughts and could follow you around, he could probably map out just where your life is heading.

According to your actions, what are you becoming? Do you have the right goals? Do you know where you are heading? Do you know what your purpose in life is and should be? What are your short-range, intermediate, and long-range goals? How does each goal fit into achieving the ultimate goal for your life? Your goals should be initially established under the careful guidance of the Holy Spirit and God's Word, using many of the principles described in this book. However, after your goals are set, you must be flexible and open to the Holy Spirit, willing to have God dynamically change your game plan at any time.

When I was aboard ship we had a navigator who would periodically take a "fix." Using celestial bodies, such as the sun, moon, and stars in conjunction with a compass, time, and tables, he could determine the exact position of our ship though we were thousands of miles from land or other recognizable objects. He knew precisely where we were, where we were going, and he could tell the helmsman the exact direction in which to steer the ship. His directions guided us through all kinds of storms and foul weather. However, periodically the navigator would take a new "fix" because changing winds, sea currents, and inaccuracies in steering would inevitably get us off course. Similarly, I believe God wants us to know where we are, where we are going, and what our course is to be. Then we must periodically take a "fix" from the Son and be willing to readjust our course accordingly.

QUESTIONS

*1. If your life could stand for only one thing—what would you want it to be? Is that what it is standing for? What do individuals in your home, at work, at church, and elsewhere see your life standing for?

*2. List your ultimate goal. Write it out.

3. List your intermediate goals. For example, these might be things that you want to accomplish in the next ten to fifteen years.

4. List short-range goals. (These might be things you are working on currently and will work on in the next few weeks, months, or possibly couple of years.)

5. Do your short-range goals lead you to your intermediate goals, and do all of them point to your ultimate goal? Are your goals realistic and practical and yet challenging?

6. Are you willing to drop or change any goal easily when directed by God?

7. If the Holy Spirit is directing us and He knows what our goals should be, why do we have to think through our goals? Why is a game plan really necessary with the Holy Spirit in our lives? How does this chapter fit with the emphasis of "now obedience"?

8. What are the problems and pitfalls of setting goals?

9. If you are going to work for a person or people in a secular or spiritual organization is it important to know the game plan and goals of those over you? Why?

THE FOLLOWING QUESTIONS ARE FOR SINGLES ONLY

10. What qualities or characteristics are absolutely necessary in a spouse? What characteristics are desirable? List.

11. Are there some qualities that should be in your life before you consider dating another person? in the person you are contemplating dating?

12. Is it necessary to date only Christians? List the reasons for and against.

13. Do you think it's necessary to know the goals of a person you might marry? Why?

PART THREE

SPECIFIC STEPS FOR KNOWING GOD'S WILL

Everything we have said in the preceding chapters regarding the nature of God's will and the prerequisites for it has an obvious bearing on knowing and living God's will. However, many people want some specific steps to follow in discerning God's will in a given matter. In part 3 I outline the specific steps as best they can be outlined from the human perspective. I have tried to arrange them in a logical order. Many of these steps have to be considered repeatedly along the way. No step can be avoided although sometimes we can quickly pass on to the next step. These are listed to help you in discerning God's will in a specific issue or decision in your life so that you are continuously living God's will.

21

STEP ONE: BE OBEDIENT TO HIS ALREADY REVEALED WILL

The primary prerequisite for knowing God's will, whether in a general or a specific issue, is obedience to His already revealed will. Many times when a person is in the place of indecision, confusion, frustration, and misfortune it is because of disobedience (*see* Deuteronomy 28:15–20; 1 Samuel 14:37). Obedience must include not only the issues at stake but also every other aspect of our lives. Psalms 66:18 in the King James Version of the Bible says, "If I regard iniquity in my heart, the Lord will not hear me" (*see also* Isaiah 59:1, 2). Proverbs 28:9 says, "If one turns away his ear from hearing the law [God's already revealed will], even his prayer is an abomination." "The LORD said to Joshua, 'Arise, why have you thus fallen upon your face?'" (Joshua 7:10). There was sin in the camp and God wanted Joshua to do something about it, not just pray. Obedient action was an absolute necessity. As mentioned earlier, Abraham's servant was led into God's will because of obedience: "I being in the way, the Lord led me . . ." (Genesis 24:27 KJV). Matthew 5:23, 24 teaches us that we may also need to get right in our relationships with other people before we can get right with God.

If God has already told you what to do about the matter, you don't need to seek the counsel of others. You don't need to study, to try and compensate with great religious acts, or even to pray about it. You *do* need to be obedient to what He has revealed (*see* Numbers 22; 1 Samuel 15:22).

Sometimes we really don't want guidance. Instead, we want to alter the will of the Guide. We don't really want to know God's will but we do want His sanction for *our* will. If we persist on this course, we will invariably end up like the children of Israel who lusted in the wilderness. God gave them their request but sent leanness into their souls (*see* Psalms 106:12–15).

The person who is obedient to God gains more and more of His special blessings and understands more about God and His will for his life (*see* Psalms 119:100). But complete obedience to what He has already revealed is fundamental to further leading regarding His will.

QUESTIONS

1. Has there ever been a time in your life where you felt God did not want you to pray any further about a matter or seek further counsel about it? Explain the details.

2. Do you think 90 percent of the problems in guidance would be solved if Christians were obedient to God's already revealed will?

*3. Right now, is there any area in your life in which you are not obedient? List.

22
STEP TWO: BE OPEN TO ANY MEANS OR RESULTS

The person who wants to know God's will in a specific area must be *open* to God's leading *in every area* of his life. He must be willing to follow God's leading *regardless of the results.* John 7:17

says, "If any man's *will is to do* his will, he shall know whether the teaching is from God . . ." (author's italics). Willingness to do His will is a prerequisite for knowing His will.

Abraham had to be *willing* to give up his most precious possession, his son; the rich young ruler, his money; the disciples, their professions. We must be *willing* to give up everything—people, food, things, money, prestige, a geographical location, for Christ (*see* Daniel 10:2, 3; Acts 13:2; Luke 9:23; John 21:18). We must be willing to undertake any profession or occupation of God's leading and be open to any change in our lives—if He should so direct.

Often the fear of what God may require is a much greater obstacle to our obedience than what God actually requires. We must be willing to give up all for Christ—but He usually only extracts a minute portion—often replacing what He has taken with something far better. To know God's will, we must have a willing heart to do anything God wants.

Also, to know God's will we must allow God to lead us *by any means* He chooses. Any preconceived idea as to how He will direct should be put aside. Naaman almost missed God's will and deliverance because of the "I thought" syndrome (*see* 2 Kings 5:11). He thought God would deliver him in a certain way—but God had a different means in mind. I wonder how often we actually prevent God from leading us because *we thought* we knew how He would do it. The Scriptures indicate this has been a major stumbling block—especially for religious people.

God has used almost every imaginable means to guide men. He has miraculously used fire, clouds, stars, and storms. Angels have appeared to men, audible voices have spoken—out of nowhere, from a burning bush, and once from a donkey. On one occasion a hand wrote His message on a wall. He has used a great fish, a dove, and a man carrying a pitcher of water. God has even used ungodly men to convey His guidance (*see* 2 Chronicles 35:20–27). His guidance has come through prophetic words, visions, dreams, and fleece. These are a few examples to emphasize that an omnipotent God may choose any means to reveal His will to you or me.

A CAUTION REGARDING MIRACULOUS GUIDANCE

Early in my Christian life I was seeking God's supernatural leading, albeit groping at times. I developed a system for determining God's will which was very logical and yet depended upon God's supernatural leading, I thought. For example, as I was driving along I would sincerely pray, "Lord, if You want me to do such and such, make the signal at the next major intersection green. If You do not want me to be involved, may it be red." This seemed logical and I thought I was basing it on spiritual principles. I must admit, however, that at times I felt uneasy about such a system. Sometimes I would reverse the sequence, looking for a confirmation of the original leading. If the two didn't agree I might even try for two out of three.

I based this system on scriptural principles taken from Gideon and his request for a sign using fleece (*see* Judges 6:36–40). Gideon wanted supernatural assurance that God truly was directing him to do a task which, humanly speaking, was sure to mean suicide. So he put out a piece of wool and asked God to cause it to be wet and the ground to be dry. When this was granted he still lacked assurance. So the next night he asked God to make the ground wet and the fleece dry. Gideon was given this confirmation. This experiment of Gideon's is similar to what we do in science in a "double-blind study." One reverses the order of things to verify the results. Gideon's incident of the fleece was truly a miracle. But often our "fleeces" are not much more than chance occurrences, though we may be a little more sophisticated than my stop-and-go-light technique. (More will be said about using "fleece" or "dictating signs" as a means of guidance in chapter 27.)

My point is that when we are attributing a supernatural-miraculous leading to God, whether it is a dream, vision, prophetic message, or any other means, we must be very careful not only that it is actually from God but also that it is actually a miraculous manifestation if we are calling it such. God usually leads in accordance with His laws of nature. When He does use personal miraculous revelation, it is typically after the usual processes have been exhausted or there are very unusual circumstances requiring His supernatural intervention.

Elijah was fed by normal means—a brook and ravens. When the brook dried up, only then did God feed him through the miracle of the bottomless containers of flour and oil. Another time Elijah performed tremendous miracles which were needed to vindicate Jehovah and Elijah as His prophet. Immediately afterward Elijah was physically exhausted and needed sleep and food. These perfectly normal human requirements were met in the usual way, though God had further business with him. But He waited until Elijah was refreshed in a normal fashion.

Some people teach that miraculous leading is the norm, an everyday occurrence. However, verses such as 1 Samuel 3:1 indicate that there are times and places where the supernatural-miraculous leading is less common. It says, "There was no frequent vision." There is no indication in passages like this that it is because of lack of faith or obedience.

Seeking miraculous leading may be an ego trip, due to unbelief or laziness (*see* Acts 8; Matthew 12:39; John 4:48; 20:20–29).

There is always a danger of introducing an authority that will compete with God's already declared Word—the Bible. In 2 Peter 1:16–21 it is indicated that the written word of God is "more sure" than visions. Thus if any guidance does not agree with the Scriptures it should be disregarded (*see* Acts 17:11; Galatians 1:6–9). This means we must study the Scriptures so we will not be caught off guard.

Remember, too, that false leaders have miraculous power. Mark 13:22 says, ". . . false prophets will . . . show signs and wonders, to lead astray. . . ." Revelation 13:11–14 tells us that the beast will be allowed to do miraculous signs in the last days. Paul warned the church in Galatians 1:6–9 that if there was even the miraculous appearance of an angel from heaven, the people must carefully check to see if anything said was contrary to the Scriptures. If there was, they were to disbelieve the supernatural appearance. Satan tried to tempt Christ to perform a miracle, to go out on a limb and expect God to intervene in a miraculous way (*see* Matthew 4). The point, then, is that miracles are not the ultimate evidence of God's guidance, though they are a means He sometimes uses (*see* Matthew 7:22, 23).

I appreciate Bob Mumford's comment on this subject. He states in *Take Another Look at Guidance*, ". . . God's Word is the final judge, and that means it *must* take precedence over our emotions, feelings, impressions, any signs or leadings we've received. *God's Word must take precedence over our subjective confidence that God has indeed spoken to us in some personal revelation.*" He quotes John Wesley: "Do not hastily ascribe things to God. Do not easily suppose dreams, voices, impressions, visions or revelations to be from God. They *may* be from Him, they *may* be from nature, they *may* be from the devil. Therefore, believe not every spirit, but try the spirits, whether they be from God."

CONCLUSION

In conclusion, then, we must be open to any means or result God has for us. We should never tell God how He should lead us or covet a method of divine guidance. Philip miraculously appeared to the eunuch when the eunuch was honestly and sincerely seeking all that God had for him from His Word. Cornelius was obedient to all the revealed Scriptures available to him. He didn't seek special supernatural guidance, but God gave it to him. Individuals who had unusual miraculous guidance in Bible times did not have the Bible as we have it today.

If we are doing what God wants us to do as revealed in His Word, and are open to Him, He will, in fact, lead us with miraculous guidance if He so chooses.

QUESTIONS

1. The author describes his simplistic stop-and-go-light technique for discerning God's will. What simplistic approaches have you used? Describe any legitimate use of "fleece" in your life or in the lives of others with whom you are familiar. What precautions are necessary when "dictating signs"?

2. Do you think refusal to admit one has been wrong is commonly a hindrance in knowing God's will among Christians? How common?

3. What steps would you take to evaluate the validity of a miracle or supernatural guidance? The following verses may help: Deuteronomy 13:1–5; 18:20–22.

4. What is the source of the material that the non-Christian dreams about? the Christian? How can one tell if a dream or vision is supernatural and inspired from God? You may want to consider Jeremiah 23:16–32; Ecclesiastes 5:3 KJV, LB; Jude verse 8; Matthew 1:20; Colossians 2:18 LB.

5. If a godly person says he has a specific prophesy from God to guide you—what should be your attitude? *See* 1 Thessalonians 5:20, 21; 1 Corinthians 14:29.

23
STEP THREE: GOD'S WORD: THE CORNERSTONE OF GUIDANCE

God's word is the single most important guide and checkpoint in our lives. It is *the* most important way to evaluate our beliefs and actions. In 2 Timothy 3:16, 17 we read, "The whole Bible was given to us by inspiration from God and is useful to teach us what is true and to make us realize what is wrong in our lives; it straightens us out and helps us do what is right" (LB). Psalms 119:105 says, "Thy Word is a lamp to my feet and a light to my path."

Many verses emphasize that God's Word is the major checkpoint for our lives. Christ verifies this in Matthew 5:18 by saying, ". . . I assure you that, while Heaven and earth last, the Law [Scriptures] will not lose a single dot or comma until its purpose is complete" (PHILLIPS). Paul further emphasizes this point in Galatians 1:6–9 by saying that even if a supernatural-miraculous appearance of an angel occurred, and the angel contradicted the already revealed will of God in the Scriptures, one should hold to the Scriptures rather than the angel's message.

The Christians at Beroea were commended in Acts 17:11 for listening to the preached Word with open and attentive hearts, then checking the Scriptures to see if what was spoken was correct. God's Word is not only our guide but it also checks error from outside of us as well as within (*see* Hebrews 4:12). But we must listen carefully to God through His Word (*see* Deuteronomy 10:12, 13).

Since the Bible is so important to us it must be part of our regular diet. In 1 Peter 2:2, 3 we read, "As newborn babes, desire the sincere milk of the word, that ye may grow thereby: If so be ye have tasted that the Lord is gracious" (KJV). God expects us to feed on His Word as our spiritual daily food. In fact, we must be saturated with it. Ignorance is never an excuse. The sincere Christian will take time to know what his Lord has to say—it is our love letter from God to us. Joshua 1:8, 9 says, "This book of the law shall not depart out of your mouth, but you shall meditate on it day and night, that you may be careful to do according to all that is written in it; for then you shall make your way prosperous, and then you shall have good success . . . for the LORD your God is with you wherever you go."

Unfortunately, a person may actually know the Scriptures *and yet not really know them.* That is, a person may *intellectually* know what the Bible says. He may have memorized it from cover to cover, and still not have *internalized* it. If he has not internalized it through obedience to it, he won't understand what the Bible is all about.

There are three steps to knowing and profiting from God's Word according to John 8:30–32, which says, "Then many of the Jewish leaders who heard him say these things began believing him to be the Messiah. Jesus said to them, 'You are truly my disciples if you live as I tell you to, and you will [only then] know the truth, and the truth will set you free' " (LB). Step one is to *hear the truth.* Step two is to *believe it.* Step three is to *live an obedient life.* The Amplified translation says, ". . . If you abide in My Word —hold fast to My teachings *and* live in accordance with them . . ." (v. 31). This is what discipleship is all about and it is the only way we will really comprehend the truth of the Scriptures.

The result of these three steps is understanding God's truth— and thus His will for our lives. This leads to truly experiencing *freedom in Christ* (*see* verse 32; *also* John 7:17). Note that full understanding only comes *after* obedience.

Our lives must be guided by His Word, checked at every point by His Word, fed by God's Word, and characterized by obedience to His Word. Then we are in a position to specifically seek God's will regarding a particular issue. We must go to the Word and specifically look for His wisdom in the matter. Suggestions on how to do this will be mentioned later. But before we consider how to correctly use God's Word in guidance, let's first consider how it is often incorrectly used.

WRONGLY USING GOD'S WORD

You have undoubtedly heard about the fellow who wanted to know God's will for his life. He prayed and asked God to direct him to his verse for the day. He then opened his large Bible and blindly put his finger upon a verse which read, "And he set his house in order, and hanged himself" (2 Samuel 17:23). This wasn't quite the verse he wanted so he decided to try for two out of three. He closed his Bible, opened it the second time, blindly put his finger on a verse, and read the following: "That thou doest, do quickly" (John 13:27 KJV).

You may say such extreme examples don't exist in real life. However, I know of an actual situation in which a Christian was having difficulty getting along with her neighbor. In her quiet time one morning, she came across "For thou shalt heap coals of fire upon his head, and the Lord shall reward thee" (Proverbs 25:22 KJV). In her mind this justified her hostility and her premeditated misdeeds against her neighbor.

However, the real difficulty comes in discerning the more subtle misuse of Scripture. The Cotton Patch Version of the New Testament refers to Satan as the "confuser." Remember how Satan misused God's Word with Eve? He even tried to misuse it with Christ. If you think you are immune to misusing God's Word or having others do it for you—forget it.

One of the biggest problems in the religious world today is the proper application of the Scriptures. This is one of the reasons there are so many cults, but it doesn't stop there. It is a problem within the ranks of born-again Christians; a problem which leads to much confusion.

Why are the Scriptures misused, you might ask? First of all, I believe there may be a deliberate attempt for self-gain. Satan certainly does this. The cults do it all the time. But unfortunately, born-again Christians are not exempt from the temptation to misuse the Scriptures for self-gain. Jeremiah 17:9, 10 says our hearts are deceitful. The clever person can, in fact, deliberately do this to prove a point. Matthew 11:19 says, ". . . But brilliant men like you can justify your every inconsistency!" (LB). Sometimes Christians are tempted to think that the end justifies the means, and misuse passages to gain their and "God's" end.

The second reason the Scriptures are misused is ignorance. Really it is a pseudoknowledge of Scripture, in most instances. For the person who is ignorant and willing to admit it, it poses no real problem. It is the person who is ignorant and either doesn't realize it, or is unwilling to admit it, who poses the problem. He may have some knowledge of the Bible but often hasn't met the qualifications described earlier in John 8:30–32. Sometimes these individuals are naive, prone to rely on "feelings of simple impressions" as Müller puts it. In other words, they have a feeling or impression which they support with a certain amount of pseudoknowledge of the Scriptures. This ultimately creates tremendous havoc for them and others.

Some Christians emphasize that we should always have an exact verse for any leading in God's will. I have read the following advice: "We must have a promise in our hand. . . . Search the Bible for some holy word which exactly fits your case. . . ." At times I believe God will give us a specific verse which is exactly applicable for our situation. However, to say that we should *always* find such a verse tends to encourage distortion and misapplication of the Scriptures. As I look at Paul's life I don't find that he had a verse to support every move he made. In fact, only seldom is this actually done in the Holy writings. This technique can give people *a false sense of security* which they think is based on the solidity of the Word of God. However, it is only as solid as *their application* of the Word of God—sometimes not very solid at all. Satan is an example of this point (*see* Matthew 4:6, 7).

PRINCIPLES IN RIGHTLY APPLYING GOD'S WORD

Every verse in the Bible is profitable for us, but not every verse in the Bible is directly applicable to us (*see* 2 Timothy 3:16, 17). In 2 Timothy 2:15 we are admonished in "rightly handling the word of truth." The Amplified translation puts it this way: ". . . correctly analyzing *and* accurately dividing—rightly handling and skillfully teaching—the Word of Truth." Let's look at some specific ways we can properly utilize God's Word.

First of all, we must learn to major on majors. There are a few major themes that run throughout the Scriptures. We must learn what they are and beware of any doctrine or practice that violates a major theme. The Pharisees, you will recall, lost sight of this and majored on the minutiae of the law. In the process they forgot about loving God and their fellow man (*see* Mark 7:1–9). The cults do this, taking an isolated verse and building a whole doctrinal system upon it.

The second point to remember in properly applying God's Word is not to overextend or make an all-inclusive application of a verse or truth. The initial truth is correct but if applied too far it goes beyond the scope the Holy Spirit intended. It's been said that "Overemphasized truth becomes a heresy." Take the example of the Sabbath, which was commanded in the Old Testament as a means of helping the people worship God and refreshing them spiritually and physically. The Pharisees extended the application of this law with so many legalistic requirements that it became a real problem. Even the disciples and Christ Himself broke the Pharisees' application of the Sabbath. You see, they didn't understand the intent of the Sabbath. By rigidly keeping this lesser commandment they actually forced people to break the first and second commandments—loving God and our fellow man.

A third point in properly applying God's Word is to remember that *some* verses are not applicable in *some* situations. They were intended for a specific situation. The story is told of a young collegian who wanted to visit Europe one summer and was looking to God for direction. He received his answer, he thought, from Acts 23:11 which says, ". . . so must thou bear witness also at Rome" (KJV). He used this to justify his going to Rome, though this command was directed specifically to Paul at a particular time and situation. We sometimes miss God's intent by not knowing the necessary *background* about a message. *When* was it written and *what was the problem* or problems? What was the *historical and cultural setting?*

The Scriptures are like love letters or like listening to one side of a conversation on the telephone—perhaps only a portion of the conversation (*see* 1 Corinthians 7:1). The Epistles especially exemplify this point. Certain facts were known and discussion had occurred between the writer and the recipient before most Epistles were written. What was written was specifically directed to a particular individual or church with its distinct situation. In fact, most of the Epistles were written to deal with a specific problem. When we understand this principle we are better able to properly apply the Scriptures.

The fourth point in the right use of the Scriptures is to understand that much of the Bible contains examples to teach us principles, rather than specific literal commands for us to follow. Please don't misunderstand me. To be sure, there are numerous specific commands that we must follow if we are to please God. However, I think it is obvious that we are not required to obey ordinances such as the sacrificial offerings of animals commanded in the Old Testament. Even though certain orders such as this are not for us to literally follow today—we can learn from them. "All these things happened to them as examples," says Paul, "as object lessons to us—to warn us against doing the same things; they were written down so that we could read about them and learn from them in these last days as the world nears its end" (1 Corinthians 10:11 LB).

The fifth point in rightly applying the Scriptures is to be sure that the qualifications for such application are both realized and met. For instance, Isaiah 55:11 in the King James Version, which indicates that God's Word "shall not return unto me void," is often quoted. But how often are the qualifications considered? I recently asked a college Sunday-school class of about seventy people how many had heard this verse used. Virtually every person raised his hand. Then I asked if anybody knew its qualifications or had ever heard them considered when the passage was used. Not one person raised his hand. Yet in the context there are several qualifications for God's Word not returning void. I personally believe that God's Word may return void when the qualifications are not met. Remember, even Satan quotes God's Word. How often do we blame God for our tragic mistakes when in reality we have simply misused the Scripture?

As just illustrated, some verses need qualification from the immediate context. At other times spiritual truths need qualification from a larger context—from all of God's Word. Let me illustrate with the subject of prayer. Christ tells us in John 16:24, "Hitherto you have asked nothing in my name; ask, and you will receive, that your joy may be full." Is the only qualification for an answer to prayer to ask in Christ's Name? If you answered solely according to this verse, you would have to say yes. But is that all the Bible says about prayer? No. Mark 11:24 says, "Whatever you ask in prayer, *believe* that you have received it, and it will be yours" (author's italics). Now there are two qualifications: Ask in Christ's Name and believe. If I search further I find a third: "If you *abide in me, and my words* abide in you, ask whatever you will, and it shall be done for you" (John 15:7 author's italics). These qualifications were given to the disciples over a period of three and a half years. James 4:3 adds a fourth qualification: "And even when you do ask you don't get it because your whole aim is wrong —you want only what will give *you* pleasure" (LB).

When you first became a Christian perhaps all God wanted you to learn was to pray in Christ's Name. As time passes He expects us to learn and apply more of the qualifications for prayer. He expects us to use the "whole counsel of God" (Acts 20:27). Another possible reason for various qualifications being given at different times is related to the specific need. The Holy Spirit was putting His finger on a certain hindrance to prayer. It may be similar to a doctor's advice to a patient—it's individual and specific. For us to properly apply God's Word to our lives requires the guidance of the Holy Spirit and our maturity so that we may be "correctly analyzing and accurately dividing . . . the Word of truth" (2 Timothy 2:15 AMPLIFIED; *see also* Hebrews 5:11–14 LB).

SEEKING GUIDANCE FROM GOD'S WORD FOR SPECIFIC DECISIONS

All that has been said so far is *essential* background material so that we may be able to rightly handle God's Word—foremost, so that we are living obediently. However, in addition we need guidance in specific matters and we *must* know what the Bible teaches about such issues. We should know any specific commands, principles, or examples that have any bearing on the matter we must decide. Start by listing all passages that come to mind that are related to the matter under consideration. Next, a concordance will help you find additional verses. This may be a small concordance in the back of your Bible or one with a more complete listing. Some Bibles have listings by topics that may be a help or there are books such as *The New Topical Text Book* that give additional references. If time permits, reading large sections of the Bible specifically looking for passages that shed light on a particular subject can yield tremendous insights and understanding of the issue. Using several translations helps immensely in clarifying passages and a good Bible dictionary is a valuable tool. Though other resources are available these will usually be sufficient. Sermons, articles, and books written on the subject may serve as an adjunct but you must be very careful to separate God's Word in them from man's interpretive ideas.

After you have listed all the passages that have any bearing on the subject, continue to pray that the Holy Spirit will help you rightly evaluate His Word. Then compare the passages. What major emphases are taught over and over? What are the qualifications? How did holy men apply the truths involved? If there seems to be a conflict, for whom was this verse specifically written? What were the circumstances of the writing? Is it applicable for us today? Is it applicable for me now? Is the way I am using it consistent with all the teachings and examples in God's Word on the subject? Do I have inward peace and assurance from the Holy Spirit with regard to the way I am using the verse? If you have an ax to grind, beware. Be careful also of proof texts—that is, trying to find verses to prove your point.

God wants to teach us His will through His Word. Understanding the necessary scriptural truths to live His will is never beyond our reach if we are honest, open, obedient, and search His Word as for hidden treasures (*see* 1 Corinthians 10:13; John 7:17; Proverbs 2:1–9).

QUESTIONS

1. Can a person expect to find God's will in a particular matter through the Scriptures if he does not study God's Word consistently at other times?

2. Do you think a person has to obey the Scriptures before he can really understand them? Is it possible to obey before you understand? Is this fair?

3. Do you think the Holy Spirit could miraculously guide you by having you open the Bible to the right verse? How often do you think He uses this method?

4. How common an occurrence among born-again Christians is misusing the Scriptures? Give a personal example with which you are familiar.

5. If we misuse the Scriptures out of ignorance, will the Holy Spirit step in and show us our mistake?

6. It's been said, "You can prove anything from the Bible." How true is this statement?

7. Does one "water down" the Scriptures by imposing too many qualifications?

8. Have you ever considered what the major themes (doctrines, emphases) are in the Bible? If you haven't, consider doing it on paper with references.

9. Do you believe God's Word ever returns void?

24
STEP FOUR: PRAYER

The person who desires to know God's will must have a life of prayer. The Scriptures clearly teach that a consistent prayer life is mandatory. Daniel prayed faithfully three times a day, the Psalmist probably seven times. It is recorded that Christ arose early in the morning to pray and at times spent hours in prayer (*see* Daniel 6:13; Psalms 119:164; Mark 1:35). (However, the Scriptures don't tell us if this was a daily occurrence with Christ.) Luther, Wesley, and saints in recent centuries reportedly spent three hours daily in prayer. Paul spoke of praying without ceasing (*see* 1 Thessalonians 5:17 KJV).

Based on information such as this there is a great tendency for Christian leaders to set guidelines for you—exactly what a life of prayer must include—times a day, length of time, and the like. To do this tends to impose another man's standards on you—often his ideals rather than what he is actually practicing day in and day out. This may help some, but it also can lead to an impossible, legalistic load, with secondary guilt and a host of other problems. On the other hand, not to be specific may encourage a prayer life that consists merely of shooting up a word of prayer as you dash out the door for work, or to pray only when in trouble or in need of God's help—not quite a life of prayer.

If you are serious about pleasing Him—and really living His will—you will have to evaluate what He expects of you at your stage of spiritual growth and in your life setting.

Beware of a prayer life characterized by "gimme prayers"; that is, give me this, give me that, do such and such. I suspect that the Lord gets very sick of the self-centered prayers that typify many of our prayer lives. Rather our prayer life should be characterized by praise and thanksgiving to Him as we express our concern for

others and God's will for their lives. With regard to ourselves—
the attitude of our prayer life, as well as the attitude of our life,
should be, "What wilt thou have me to do?" and "Teach me to
do thy will" and "May he give us the desire to do his will in
everything" (Acts 9:6 KJV; Psalms 143:10; 1 Kings 8:58 LB).

An integral part of a life of prayer is not so much asking or even
talking to God but listening and meditation. Much of God's will
is learned in precisely this way. Isaiah 41:1 says, "Listen to me in
silence . . . let them approach, then let them speak. . . ." The
Psalmist says, ". . . the meditation of my heart shall be understanding" (Psalms 49:3).

Meditation is not a luxury. It is a basic necessity. I doubt if any
person can really know God and His will without meditation, not
only when he needs some specific guidance—but it also should
be a prime characteristic of his life. The first step to knowing
God's will for the zealous Christian moving at a frantic pace is to
stop and prayerfully meditate.

In addition to a life of prayer and meditation the Bible teaches
us to pray specifically when we want to know His will about a
particular matter. "If you want to know what God wants you to
do, *ask him,* and he will gladly tell you . . ." (James 1:5 LB author's
italics). Proverbs 3:6 commands us, "In all thy ways acknowledge
him, and he shall direct thy paths" (KJV). Müller learned by experience to "Ask God in prayer to reveal His will to me aright."

A tragic violation of this principle is recorded in Joshua 9. God
had specifically commanded the Israelites not to make covenants
with nearby countries. However, the Hivites had heard how God
had destroyed other countries through the Israelites and they
feared for their own safety. So they sent ambassadors requesting
a peace treaty. Their method, however, was one of trickery. The
ambassadors arrived wearing old, worn-out clothes and carrying
moldy food. Joshua asked the right question, were they from a far
country? But the ambassadors lied and the Scriptures say that
"Joshua and the other leaders finally believed them. *They did not
bother to ask the Lord,* but went ahead and signed a peace treaty"

(Joshua 9:14, 15 LB author's italics). Therefore, even though Joshua evaluated the situation, he failed to ask God specifically about the matter. His oversight plagued the Israelites with difficulties for years to come. Therefore, to pray specifically to God regarding His will in a matter cannot be overemphasized. If we would know His will, we *must ask Him His will.* This should be done during our protracted times of prayer and preferably several different times for any important decision. But if an unexpected decision comes up it's appropriate to follow the advice of King Jehoshaphat when he said, "However, let's check with the Lord first" (2 Chronicles 18:4 LB). It's a good thing that he did, as his immediate impulse was contrary to God's will.

There are a few situations, however, in which prayer may be the wrong thing. Let me touch on these. Proverbs 28:9 says, "If one turns away his ear from hearing the law, even his prayer is an abomination." If God has specifically indicated what you should do, to pray further about it may be a sin. Although Joshua failed to pray when he should have in Joshua 9, in the seventh chapter God told him, "Get up off your face!" (verse 10 LB). There was sin in the camp and action needed to be taken. Prayer was not needed. Prayer is never a substitute for appropriate action.

Prayer may even be a disguise for rejecting God's will or it may be used as a means to covet. I have personally been guilty of this (*see* Psalms 106:14, 15). Moses had to learn this lesson. In Deuteronomy 3:25 he specifically asked God to let him enter the Promised Land. God initially planned that he would enter the Promised Land, but because of sin Moses was denied this privilege. However, Moses continued to ask God about it—if you will, to beg God. Finally God said, "Speak no more to me of this matter" (verse 26).

We tend to pray about the things that are important to us excessively. At other times we fail to pray enough about things that are vitally important to God. This should be corrected. The point remains, however, that if we would know His will we must pray and ask Him His will. This may vary from a moment of prayer when confronted with the need for an immediate decision, to times of protracted prayer and meditation regarding His will in the matter.

QUESTIONS

*1. What guidelines do you believe God wants you to follow in your prayer life:

    (a) How often should you have planned prayer?

    (b) How long a time should you pray during these times?

    (c) Is there any special time of day you believe you should pray?

2. Have you ever used prayer lists? What is their place and value?

3. What does it mean to "pray without ceasing" (1 Thessalonians 5:17 KJV)? I know a person who says he prays before every sentence he speaks—is this the ideal? How small a matter should you pray about—the tie or dress you wear, etc.?

4. How do we know when God would have us stop praying about an issue as opposed to praying with "importunity" (*see* Luke 11:5–13; 18:1–7)?

25
STEP FIVE: THE HOLY SPIRIT

To know God's will we must not only acknowledge the person of the Holy Spirit but also allow Him to control our lives. Christ tells us that the Holy Spirit is given to every believer (*see* John 14:16, 17; Romans 8:14). However, we are further told, in fact commanded, that we should be filled with the Holy Spirit (*see* Ephesians 5:18). God wants to fill us with the Holy Spirit as we allow Him to control more areas of our life. We can have as much of Him as we really want.

Personally, I don't think it is too important whether the filling of the Holy Spirit comes through a dramatic, instantaneous moment of yielding, with some external manifestation, or through a more gradual yielding (*see* Romans 6:13–16). The important question is, *Are you filled now?* I find that although I am filled with the Holy Spirit on one day, the pressures of life take their toll. I must take the time and effort to continually reopen my life to God through His Word, prayer, meditation, obedience, and an awareness of the Holy Spirit within me. This is the means for me to have the overflowing of the Holy Spirit in my life. It's a tremendous realization to know that God's Spirit is within our lives.

One of the major purposes of the Holy Spirit is to be a counselor, teacher, and guide. John 14:16 tells us that the Holy Spirit will be our Counselor. John 14:26 says, "He will teach you all things." John 16:13 says, "He will guide you into all the truth." The Holy Spirit is our constant Guide in our moment-by-moment relationship with God and the world. He is the One who brings it all together. He is our personal adviser about life's daily decisions and problems; thus fulfilling God's will in our life. The Holy Spirit's guidance, if based on God's Word, is the checkpoint that the guidance we receive is from God and not from self or other spirits. George Müller says again on this subject, "I seek the will of the Spirit of God through or in connection with the Word of God. The Spirit and the Word must be combined." The Holy Spirit is never grieved when we honestly check to see that a message is consistent with the Word of God. In fact, we are commanded, "Do not believe every spirit, but test the spirits to see whether they are of God" (1 John 4:1). The Holy Spirit directs us in our personal application of the Scriptures. Apart from Him we would not know how to make this application correctly.

J. I. Packer aptly warns us in *Knowing God* that one can slip into error if he tries to depend on the Holy Spirit to the exclusion of God's Word and personal responsibility. He says:

The idea of a life in which the inward voice of the Spirit decides and directs everything sounds most attractive, for it seems to exalt the Spirit's ministry and to promise the closest intimacy with God; but in practice this quest for superspirituality leads only to frantic bewilderment or lunacy. Hannah Whitall Smith . . . tells of the woman who each morning, having consecrated the day to the Lord as soon as she woke, 'would then ask Him whether she was to get up or not,' and would not stir till 'the voice' told her to dress. 'As she put on each article she asked the Lord whether she was to put it on, and very often the Lord would tell her to put on the right shoe and leave off the other; sometimes she was to put on both stockings and no shoes; and sometimes both shoes and no stockings; it was the same with all the articles of dress . . .' Then there was the invalid who, when her hostess, visiting her, left money by accident on the dressing-table, had 'an impression that the Lord wanted her to take that money in order to illustrate the truth of the text that "all things are yours" '— which she did, and hid it under her pillow, and prevaricated when her hostess came back for it, and was eventually thrown out as a thief . . . (*Group Movements*, pp. 184, 245, 198). These pathetic stories are sadly typical of what ensues once the basic mistake about guidance has been made. What conduct of this sort shows is failure to grasp that the fundamental mode whereby our rational Creator guides His rational creatures is by rational understanding and application of His written Word.

How does the Holy Spirit lead us? Sometimes He leads through supernatural-miraculous methods discussed earlier in chapter 22. This means may be a voice, a vision, a dream, etc. However, in my opinion the far more common way He leads is in a deep, inward assurance that a given thing is God's will. This is exemplified in Luke 2:27 which says, "The Holy Spirit had impelled him to go . . ." (LB). There is a deep sense of oughtness or rightness that we should do a certain thing and that it is in no way contrary to the Scriptures. This assurance is accompanied by a deep sense of peace. Exodus 33:14 says, "My presence will go with you, and I will give you rest." This peace which accompanies our obedience to the leading of the Holy Spirit is so important that I am devoting an entire chapter to it (chapter 30). This deep peace which comes from the Holy Spirit is in sharp contrast to our emotional feelings or impulses. Often these emotional feelings are accompanied by an impulse to hurry and get the job done and an emotional feeling of unrest.

The Holy Spirit's leading is always consistent with the Scriptures and enlightened reason and judgment. From the eternal perspective it makes sense.

Many times God has led me through this deep, inward prodding of the Holy Spirit. Probably the most vivid example happened many years ago when I was in the service. I was in electronics school with thousands of other servicemen attending various schools on Treasure Island. There was a certain fellow who was in a different class and whom I only vaguely knew, yet he kept coming to mind. I had the deep impulse that I should share Christ with him. Finally, one day I went out of my way to sit down with him and share the Gospel. Somewhat to my amazement he was wide open to the Gospel and eagerly responded to Christ. Many years have passed now and he is continuing in his Christian life. Such a deep, inward conviction is the Holy Spirit impelling us to do His will.

QUESTIONS

1. Could a person be dramatically baptized with the Holy Spirit and not be filled with the Spirit today?

2. If the Holy Spirit wants to be our personal Guide, why do we need to consider all the other steps in knowing God's will?

3.   How would you describe the Holy Spirit's internal leading in your life? Give some examples.

4.   Do you believe a feeling of rightness may exist in people when they are actually wrong? (*See* Proverbs 14:12; 16:2.) How can one tell if his feeling of rightness is from God? Is this only a problem for non-Christians?

5.   How would you define *enlightened reason* and *judgment* and *the eternal perspective*?

26
STEP SIX: COUNSEL

Our primary counsel regarding God's will should come from God Himself through the Word of God. However, there are times when God uses the counsel of other people to help us know His will. The writer of Proverbs knew the value of good counselors when he wrote:

Where no counsel is, the people fall: but in the multitude of counsellors there is safety.

Proverbs 11:14 KJV

Without counsel plans go wrong, but with many advisers they succeed.

Proverbs 15:22

He that hearkeneth unto counsel is wise.

Proverbs 12:15 KJV

Get all the advice you can and be wise the rest of your life.

Proverbs 19:20 LB

The aim of counsel should be clearly understood. In some instances it is primarily to gain information. A student seeks advice from a school counselor regarding classes and requirements for certain courses. You go to a physician to correct a health problem. This is something I would highly recommend if there is any question of a medical problem.

Another reason for seeking counsel is to make sure you don't have a blind spot—an area you are grossly overlooking which a counselor can quickly spot. At other times we seek counsel to help us clarify our thoughts. Thus the counselor should be a sympathetic person who is willing to listen. He may ask some provocative questions but will not be too quick to jump in with solutions. Another reason for seeking counsel is to help you avoid impulsive emotional decisions.

Now let me give you some counsel regarding counseling.

1. We should probably never seek or listen to counsel from men if the Counselor (God) has already spoken on the subject. King Amaziah didn't like God's counsel given to him through God's prophet, so he sought his own counselors. Consequently he disobeyed God and died as a result (*see* 2 Chronicles 25:16). There are times when God may specifically direct us not to seek counsel. Paul, you will remember, went into the desert and specifically avoided the counsel of Christ's disciples (*see* Galatians 1:16–19).

2. On the other hand, sometimes seeking counsel from others is God's appointed means for revealing His will to us. Proverbs 10:8 says, "The wise man is glad to be instructed, but a self-sufficient fool falls flat on his face" (LB). Pride keeps many people from seeking help from others and may ultimately prevent them from knowing God's will. Naaman's pride almost kept him from experiencing God's healing (*see* 2 Kings 5). The Gentile Cornelius had to get counsel from the Jew Peter to obtain God's full message (*see* Acts 10). The treasurer of

Ethiopia needed Philip's explanation of the Scriptures for salvation (*see* Acts 8). Joshua was the chosen leader after Moses, yet he had to learn God's will through the priest Eleazar (*see* Numbers 27:20–23).

3. It is important to seek counsel from the right individuals. Some people run from one person to another seeking advice. Chances are they just want to talk about their problems and indecision and really aren't seeking counsel at all. Others seek advice only from those who will condone what they have already decided to do.

   Seek counsel from one or two individuals who are emotionally and spiritually mature. In most instances they should know you and the area of your concern. Avoid individuals whose blind spots coincide with yours. They should be willing to say "I don't know" if they cannot help you and be willing to qualify any advice given as Paul did: "I give my opinion. . . . I have no command of the Lord. . . . And I think that I have the Spirit of God" (1 Corinthians 7:12–40 RSV, KJV). Do not choose people who have an ax to grind or any vested interest in the matter under consideration. They will not be able to give you objective advice. The counselor must not have any preconceived ideas as to God's will for your life. His prime concern must be to help you know God's will, not to maintain a program of other concerns that are merely *his* will. He must be willing to have you decide that God's will is different than he thinks—and not pressure you in the process.

4. Be careful of the wrong counsel. Psalms 1:1 warns us about obtaining counsel from the wicked. However, even well-meaning friends at times may give us the wrong advice. The counsel of Job's friends, you will recall, was unsolicited and very ill-advised. The ten spies gave the wrong counsel to the children of Israel and it cost them forty more years in the dry, parched desert.

Paul warns us that though we start out well, the wrong persuasion can adversely affect our entire life. This influence can come unconsciously through dynamic, powerful, gifted personalities or movements. We must guard against being motivated by such means without *full* confidence that it's God's will through all the other means described in God's Word (*see* 1 Corinthians 2:1–5; Galatians 1:6–8).

Sometimes even Christian leaders are capable of giving us the wrong counsel. Peter was in the wrong when he compelled Gentiles to live like Jews (*see* Galatians 2:1–14). We are warned that even if leaders claim "They have seen a vision . . . and know you should" do such and such, they still *may* be wrong. We are advised to refuse such counsel (*see* 1 Kings 13; Colossians 2:16–18 LB; Galatians 1:6–9). If the counsel doesn't agree with the Scriptures and enlightened reason and doesn't have the sanction of the peace of the Holy Spirit, you have ample cause to disregard it (*see* Nehemiah 6:10–13; Isaiah 8:20 KJV).

Many times throughout my life I have received the counsel of Christian leaders, and much of the advice has been good. However, a few times the advice of Christian leaders whom I highly respect has proven to be wrong. On one occasion I sought the counsel of a Christian leader regarding a particular girl I wanted to date. She had many of the qualities I felt a Christian girl should have. Even though this counselor knew both of us, he advised against my dating her. Thus it was another four years until my first date with the girl I eventually married. Though I respected the man's judgment in most matters, after sixteen happy years of marriage I feel certain his advice was dead wrong!

When you go to someone for advice, remember that the ultimate decision is yours, not the counselor's. Don't expect someone else to make the decisions for which God holds you responsible. Romans 14:5 says, "Let every one be fully convinced *in his own mind*" (author's italics).

QUESTIONS

1. What might cause a Christian leader to give you the wrong counsel? (*See* 2 Corinthians 11:14; 1 Kings 13:18.)

2. Do you think a young Christian is more likely to need counsel than an older Christian? a woman more than a man? an emotionally unstable person more than an emotionally stable person?

3. Should a marriage counselor, psychologist, or psychiatrist ever be consulted? Must they be born-again Christians? (*Consider* 2 Chronicles 35:17–23; 1 Corinthians 2:14.)

4. Does anyone very often positively know God's will for another person?

5. A friend of yours says to you, "Joe, you ought to come to the Wednesday-night Bible study." Is he implying he knows God's will for your life? Is this a subtle form of manipulation we should avoid?

6. How do you know from whom you should seek counsel and when you should seek counsel?

27
STEP SEVEN: PROVIDENTIAL CIRCUMSTANCES

A donkey that "strayed away" and an off-the-cuff statement by Saul's servant, who said, "I've just thought of something," were the means God used to guide Saul to a feast where he was anointed king (*see* 1 Samuel 9 LB).

A rebellious queen set the stage for Esther, through her grace and beauty, to be chosen queen of the Median and Persian Em-

pire. Later the king's sleepless night led to his reading the right
portion of a historical record telling of the uncovering of an
assassination attempt. These were all key circumstances in the
deliverance of God's people from total annihilation. No *apparent
miraculous intervention,* but a series of *Providential circumstances* were
God's means of guidance and deliverance (*see* Book of Esther).

We see God's guidance in Joseph's life. His brothers wanted
to kill him but decided to throw him into a deep hole in the
ground that "just happened" to be nearby. Then a caravan to
Egypt "just happened" by and Joseph was sold to the traders. A
certain job, a satisfied employer, a revengeful woman, prison, the
right acquaintances, dreams, and a famine, plus much time—
were all further means God used in leading Joseph to his position
of second in command in all of Egypt. I wonder if Joseph had any
idea that the circumstances of his life were part of God's providential guidance? But after many years and in retrospect, he
could say to his brothers, ". . . God did it! He sent me here ahead
of you to preserve your lives. . . . God turned into good what you
meant for evil, for he brought me to this high position I have
today so that I could save the lives of many people" (Genesis
45:5; 50:20 LB).

We read in 1 Samuel of David, a shepherd boy carrying food
supplies to his brothers in battle. This led to his confrontation
with Goliath, resulting in Israel's victory over the Philistine army.

There is no end to the examples in Scripture of how God has
used circumstances in guiding His people. And I can personally
attest that Providential circumstances have a part in the small and
large decisions of my life.

Before we go any further let's define our terms. Webster
defines *circumstances* as a condition, fact, event, or state of affairs.
Circumstances are just what's happening around us—things over
which we have little or no control. *Providential* refers to divine
direction or foresight. It also conveys the thought of being fortunate, prudent, and opportune. Therefore we can define *Providential circumstances* as the natural-appearing events in our environ-

ment that God specifically arranged or is using to guide us. These become opportunities in our lives. However, to turn Providential circumstances into divine opportunities often requires our initiative.

In the incidents of Saul being led to his anointing and Joseph's pilgrimage, the Providential circumstances led them without much initiative or evaluation required on their part. They were more or less forced into situations. However, Providential circumstances often open doors of opportunity that we must evaluate and for which we must take appropriate action if God's desired results are to be achieved. Esther exemplifies this, as does Paul's finding doors opening for him to preach the Gospel (*see* Esther 4; 1 Corinthians 16:9; 2 Corinthians 2:12).

DIVINE CONFIRMATION

There is another way God gives guidance that involves Providential circumstances plus an additional confirmation, indicator, or evidence. The indicator itself is not a miraculous act such as Gideon's dictated sign but otherwise has similarities with his confirmation by fleece. For example, there were probably scores of men every day carrying jars of water into Jerusalem—that was no miracle—but Christ's directions to His disciples were, "As soon as you enter Jerusalem, you will see a man walking along carrying a pitcher of water. Follow him into the house he enters. . . . That is the place" (Luke 22:10–12 LB). This is divine leading through natural means. Then there was Jonathan, who wasn't sure if the Lord was leading him and his bodyguard against an opposing army. They decided, "This is what we will do. . . . When they see us, if they say, 'Stay where you are or we'll kill you!' then we will stop and wait for them. But if they say, 'Come on up and fight!' then we will do just that; for it will be *God's signal* that he will help us defeat them!" (1 Samuel 14:8–12 LB author's italics). God gave the requested signal and victory to Jonathan.

Abraham's servant needed guidance in obtaining the right wife for Isaac and so prayed, "May the right one do such and such," and God started fulfilling his request before he had finished praying (*see* Genesis 24:10–26). It should be emphasized that Abraham's servant was following instructions, was responsible, had a tremendous faith in God—was doing all the other things necessary in order to be led by God. He said of himself, "I being in the way, the Lord led me . . ." (Genesis 24:27 KJV).

Requesting divine confirmation should probably only be used when other means have not yielded an answer or when one needs additional assurance. Guidance by Providential circumstances or divine confirmation must never be an "easy out" or means to avoid essential prerequisites and steps in guidance. These means could easily be misused—resulting in what you *think* is God guiding you—but which is really nothing more than your own or chance direction.

In the past I have avoided using divine confirmation in guidance, probably due to my bad experience with the stop-and-go-light technique (*see* chapter 22) and for fear of misusing this means. However, recently I used it and believe it was of God. It involved my change in professional fields, which I mentioned in an earlier chapter. So far as I could discern it was God's will that I switch from internal medicine to psychiatry, which meant going back to a teaching hospital for three additional years of on-the-job training. It seemed the move should be made the following July and should to be one of three hospitals. After I left the interviews of the first two hospitals I had an awful inward feeling that they were not for me (there were also some factual matters that concerned me). This somewhat threw me—I asked myself, Why should I feel so negative about these two hospitals if God is really leading me to a change? *What if I feel the same way after the third interview?* Was I wrong about making a change in fields of practice? Eventually I made the last appointment. Before I went I prayed, "Lord, if You are in this change may You: (1) give me a positive inward reassurance that the change is of You and this is the hospital in which I should do my residency; (2) may they receive me heartily and offer me a position; (3) may they pay me on the fourth-year salary level instead of the first-year level which is the level of training I will be in." God graciously granted each part of my request including the one for divine confirmation.

WARNINGS ABOUT CIRCUMSTANCES

Once there was an all-powerful king who happened to be resting on his palace roof, and the circumstances were such that he saw a very beautiful woman. He had full power to have her brought to him and to have an affair (*see* 2 Samuel 11). But they certainly weren't Providential circumstances—it was not God's will that he take advantage of the opportunity that circumstances afforded him. Jonah was fleeing Ninevah and went to the seacoast and *happened* to find a ship ready to sail in the opposite direction and *fortunately* he had enough money for a ticket. Again, the availability of these circumstances had nothing to do with God's will or direction in his life. Circumstances are just the state of things around us. They may be providential, they may be indifferent, or they may even be an avenue that leads to sin. Eve's circumstances allowed her to easily take of the fruit in the garden—which was not God's will. *Therefore, we must never be led by circumstances alone.* They are only one of a series of factors to consider.

Seemingly bad circumstances, on the other hand, may not be God's closing doors. The Bible is filled with difficult situations that God's people had to overcome in order to follow God's will. The journey of the children of Israel and the struggles of Nehemiah exemplify this point.

However, adverse circumstances may be providential warnings. God used a rebellious donkey to warn Balaam to be careful (*see* Numbers 22). He used a storm and a great fish as a warning to Jonah, thus allowing a new opportunity for obedience. Tension or adverse situations may be God's guidance to leave a situation (*see* Genesis 31; Acts 9:25).

Therefore, if we run into trouble—especially if there are repeated difficulties—it should cause us to stop and reevaluate whether or not we are really in God's will. We usually don't have to force open God's doors of opportunity.

CONCLUSION

My aim has not been to confuse you by presenting the pros and cons of the role of circumstances in our lives. I certainly believe God does use, as one form of guidance, Providential circumstances. However, we must be careful not to overuse or rely on this method. Circumstances are the facts of life around us—if we don't fully consider them we aren't using our God-given brain. George Müller says, "Take into account Providential circumstances." To me, that is the point—to carefully consider and evaluate the opportunities God is presenting to us *in light of all the other considerations in this book.* How to evaluate properly is the topic of our next chapter.

"Be most careful then how you conduct yourselves: like sensible men, not like simpletons. Use the *present opportunity* to the full . . . try to understand what the will of the Lord is" (Ephesians 5:15–17 NEB author's italics).

QUESTIONS

1. If circumstances can be good, bad, or indifferent, something to yield to or a warning to avoid—how are they useful at all in knowing God's will?
2. Give a personal example of God leading you through Providential circumstances.

28
STEP EIGHT: EVALUATION

A middle-aged patient of mine was having recurrent chest pain. A lung scan revealed that she had blood clots in her lungs. The patient was hospitalized and her blood was "thinned." She did fairly well and was discharged after a couple of weeks. I continued to follow her as an outpatient and kept her blood "thinned."

Over the ensuing months, however, the chest pains continued and she was reevaluated a number of times. Some radiologists and other consultants felt she had new clots in her lungs, others did not. This posed a problem for me as her primary physician. I thought, If new clots are going to her lungs the next step in treatment is to tie off (block) the major returning vein from her legs to her heart. This often results in swelling of the legs and pain, and is no guarantee that a new clot will not someday hit the lungs. If the vein is not tied, a large clot could be fatal. As her physician what should I do?

Tough decisions like this occur every day in medicine. I am acutely aware that how I make these decisions has a tremendous effect upon my patients. In our daily lives, however, we often fail to realize that the decisions we make have tremendous ramifications for our lives and the lives of others. Proper evaluation is crucial for making decisions—not only in medicine but also in all the decisions of life.

In some situations evaluation can be made in a fraction of a second. In more difficult situations evaluation takes time. Careful evaluation requires that we (1) have all the necessary information; (2) be willing to consider the factors for and against a given decision and the source and importance of each factor; (3) consider the effects of whatever decision we make. *Careful evaluation must include all the major guideposts discussed earlier in this book:* an *openness* to any means of God's leading including the miraculous; an awareness of what *God's Word* says on the subject; openness to the *Holy Spirit's* leading; *praying* for His guidance; seeking *counsel* if needed; and the consideration of *Providential circumstances.* However, "His voice" from all sources should always agree—that is, the Scriptures, promptings from the Holy Spirit, and any miraculous leading from God. In the final analysis, God's written Word—the Bible—must always remain the cornerstone of guidance.

The scriptural basis for evaluation is woven throughout the Bible. Samuel told Saul, "At that time the Spirit of the Lord will come mightily upon you. . . . From that time on your decisions should be based on whatever seems *best under the circumstances,* for the Lord will guide you" (1 Samuel 10:6, 7 LB). The writer of Hebrews admonishes that, ". . . solid food is for full-grown men, for those whose senses and *mental faculties are trained by practice to discriminate and distinguish* between what is morally good and noble and what is evil and contrary either to divine or human law" (Hebrews 5:14 AMPLIFIED, italics author's).

Phillips puts it this way: ". . . the man who has developed by experience his power to *discriminate* between what is good and what is bad for him." Paul further states, "The spiritual man judges all things . . ." (1 Corinthians 2:15). The Amplified Version says it this way: "But the spiritual man tries all things—[that is] he examines, investigates, inquires into, questions, and *discerns* all things . . ." (italics author's).

Once we begin to evaluate, Satan will try to confuse the issues. One way he does this is to encourage us to rely on our feelings. A feeling is a strong inner leaning toward something. The basis of that feeling may be good or bad, for our feelings are the result of a lifetime of various internal and external stimuli. This may include mixed-up emotions, impure motives, prejudices, or old thought patterns.

There are four sources of impressions: God, Satan, other people, and our own feelings. God's voice is always good, so that is no problem. Satan is always bad. That would be no problem if we always recognized his workings. However, he usually disguises himself through people, pressures, etc. Therefore, most of the loud voices we hear are either from within—our own desires and impressions—or from people about us. In either case, these impressions may be good or bad. We have many legitimate desires and needs that should be considered. On the other hand, our hearts may be deceitful and sinful (*see* Jeremiah 17:1-10). People may help us or they may manipulate and use us for their own selfish ends, even in spiritual things. The pressure to please people is also a problem (*see* the chapter "People-Pleasing" in *Run and Not Be Weary* by the author). We want to gain their favor. And there is tremendous pressure to help keep the machinery of churches and organizations running. This may be good or bad. The point I am trying to make is that, because of the many pressures upon us, feelings or impressions alone are not a sufficient basis for a decision.

Remember, even if the matter you are considering is good, scriptural, and desperately needed, it does not necessarily mean God is calling *you* to pursue that course of action—at least at this time. Any action you undertake must not only be of God but *He also must want you to do it at this time.*

Be willing to suspect yourself—your motives and feelings in a matter. However, realize that if you are yielded to Him, often God's will comes through your own desires.

Be careful about undertaking evaluation on any important decision when you are tired. Your thought processes and decisions can be adversely affected by fatigue. God had Elijah first get plenty of sleep and adequate nourishment before He revealed His will further to him (*see* 1 Kings 19:4-15; *see also* Mark 6:31). Whenever possible avoid making "on the spot" decisions, even about small things. Get alone and give yourself time to prayerfully consider the matter before God. Rarely are immediate decisions really necessary. If someone is pressuring you—that should raise your suspicion about the matter—though it may still be God's will for you.

Recently I was asked to be on a steering committee for a good
Christian work. It would only have involved possibly four to ten
hours of my time, but it was one of those decisions about which
I felt much ambivalence. Something within me said, "Yes, go,"
and something else said, "No, don't go." I was willing to do
whatever God wanted, but for a long time I wasn't sure what God
wanted me to do.

To resolve the problem I decided to take a good look at my
reasons for getting involved or not getting involved.

On one side of a piece of paper I listed my reasons for involvement. On the other side I listed reasons for not being involved.
I considered the importance of each reason and gave it a percentage figure accordingly. My list looked like this:

YES (Reasons for Involvement)	NO (Reasons Not to Be Involved)
1. To show my interest and support of the work.(10%)	1. Probably only busy work—I doubt if anything much of eternal significance will result.(50%)
2. This committee may produce some good spiritual results.(10%)	2. Other heavy commitments to God's work, family, medical practice, etc. (50%)
3. What will they think of me if I don't go and support them? (80%)	

As I laid the matter before the Lord it became obvious that 80
percent of my reasons for involvement was, "What will they think
of me if I don't go and support them?" The Holy Spirit used this
to show me that I should not get involved. I have found over and
over that this system works as I seek to clarify underlying motives
and God's will for me.

As you consider alternatives do not rush into a decision. Meditate on the facts, prayerfully asking God's will. Meditation helps
clarify the sources of our feelings and solidify a decision.

When King Hezekiah received a distressing letter he "went up to the house of the LORD, and spread it before the LORD." He prayed, allowed God to help clarify the issues, and God answered his prayer (*see* 2 Kings 19:14–21). Making important decisions alone with God without any pressure is crucial.

Evaluation is that essential part of divine guidance where we bring together the various means of evidence, consider the weight of each, and allow the Holy Spirit to enlighten our understanding so that we might make the right choice in determining God's will.

QUESTIONS

1. Describe how you have evaluated issues and come to appropriate conclusions in discerning God's will in your life. Have you ever written the pros and cons on a sheet of paper? How did it work for you? What other suggestions would you add?

2. To what extent should God's will for us be determined if another is offended by the course of action we take? (*See* Romans 14:14–23; Galatians 2:11; 1 Corinthians 10:23.) Have you ever seen this teaching abused? Explain. How would you properly qualify this teaching?

Note: For the sake of completeness and to prevent misunderstanding, a comment should be made regarding Scriptures referring to lot-casting or "throwing sacred dice."

During one period in Old Testament history the high priest used the "Urim and Thummim" to discern God's will. These were some type of special objects—possibly stones—that were able to give a yes-or-no answer, or fail to give an answer at all. In the New Testament there is only one incident of lot-casting and that was in choosing a replacement for Judas. Matthias, who was chosen by this method, is never mentioned again in the Scriptures and many Bible scholars question the appropriateness of the disciples' action. They believe Paul was the twelfth disciple "born out of due time" (1 Corinthians 15:8 KJV).

On one occasion George Müller tried this method and became disillusioned with it, concluding it was not for our age.

I likewise do not believe lot-casting, flipping a coin, drawing straws, or any other means of chance decision-making has a place in discerning God's will for our lives (*see* Exodus 28:30; Numbers 27:21; Joshua 14:1–3; 1 Samuel 28:6; 1 Chronicles 24:5; Acts 1:23–26).

29
STEP NINE: THE DECISION: TO WAIT OR TO ACT

After having taken the previous eight steps in determining God's will in a matter the time arrives to *decide to wait* or to *decide to act*. There must be an active choice. Not to decide is to decide. No choice—is a choice. Indecision will lead to a choice by default —which is a poor choice.

If a person's heart is basically right before God and he prayerfully makes a choice that is wrong—that may at times be better than the choices made by the person who is constantly in a state of indecision. One should never take responsibility in knowing God's will and making the right decision lightly. However, God has occasionally intervened when the wrong decision was made by a person living God's will—but we should never rely on such intervention (*see* 2 Samuel 7:1–4).

Good decision-making has several characteristics. It involves obtaining the necessary facts and evaluation as discussed in the previous chapters. When it involves the will of God it necessitates personal obedience.

As discussed earlier, the evaluation and decision should be made alone—away from pressures of time or people if at all possible. It's ideal and usually possible to prayerfully make the decision and then "sit on" it. That is, decide what your course of action should be but delay implementing it for a while. The period of delay may vary from a few minutes to hours, days, or occasionally years. You may want to share your decision with a confidant but it's best not to tell others of your decision immediately. If you do it's a lot more difficult to alter that decision later (*see* Nehemiah 1, 2). This period of delay gives the Holy Spirit time to reaffirm the correctness of the decision; or if it's out of God's will, He will cause you to be uneasy and allow the opportunity of changing the decision (more will be said about this point in the next chapter).

George Müller said, "I come to deliberate judgment according to the best of my ability and knowledge and if my mind is thus at peace and continues so after two or three more petitions, I proceed accordingly." In another place he says, "Be slow to take new steps in the Lord's service, or in your business, or in your families. Weigh everything well."

Balaam properly waited overnight before giving his decision (*see* Numbers 22). Impetuous decisions are usually the wrong ones (*see* Mark 9:1–7; John 21:3 KJV).

Isaiah 28:16 says, "He who believes will not be in haste." Proverbs 19:2 says, "It is dangerous and sinful to rush into the unknown" (LB).

Earlier I discussed my professional change. This decision was made while on a short vacation. I told my wife of the deep inner conviction which I believed to be of God. However, I did not tell any other person for a year but prayerfully considered the matter before God. It was a full three years before I made public my decision and signed the contract. It should be noted that this was not procrastination. It was "sitting on" the decision. However, we must never let "sitting" become procrastination.

WAIT BEFORE YOU DECIDE

Sometimes when we come to the point of decision God's answer is "Wait." "Wait for My direction." It's premature to either know or act on the issue. Marriage is often a good example of this. A young person may be very anxious to know "who" is God's will and "when." To both of these questions God may be saying, "Wait and trust Me." We may have to choose not to worry or even spend a lot of time thinking about the matter. We may even have to stop praying about a matter for a time. Guidance delayed is not guidance denied. When the guidance is needed God will give it if we are living an obedient life. It may mean that we will have to reevaluate at a later date the steps listed previously—but now we are to wait. In decisions of this category often time will easily clarify God's will. If you are confused or uneasy it may be God saying, "Wait and trust."

WAIT FOR THE FULFILLMENT

Sometimes God has revealed His will to us but the time of fulfillment is unknown. Saul wasn't willing to wait a *full* seven days as required by the Lord. This sin cost his descendants the dynasty (*see* 1 Samuel 13). There are many scriptural examples of *seeming* delays in God's fulfilling His will and promises. Abraham had to wait twenty-three years for his promised son. David waited many years between the time he was anointed king at God's command and the time he became king. During the interval his life was constantly endangered, yet he refused to take matters into his own hands. A delay in fulfillment doesn't mean God isn't concerned or that He is failing to guide.

DECIDE TO ACT

Sometimes God's decision is no—if that is the case we must accept it without complaint.

On the other hand, God's will may be for us to proceed or take action. Sometimes this may be somewhat difficult. It may require risks. But there comes a time when failure to act is sin. Moses was told by God, "Why do you cry to me? Tell the people of Israel to go forward. Lift up your rod, and stretch out your hand over the sea . . ." (Exodus 14:15–16).

There came a time in my recent deliberations regarding occupation when I felt God wanted me to act. I had made the decision and waited three years with constant peace that the professional change was of God. But to make the change meant giving up a certain amount of security—there was a risk and a price to pay. This had to be overcome by my actively taking the necessary steps without further delay. At a certain point in time I had to act—not too soon, and not too late.

Therefore, we must actively choose God's will. That choice may be (1) to wait further before God will reveal His will; (2) to wait until God will fulfill His will; (3) to accept His answer of no; (4) for you to decide to actively implement His will.

QUESTIONS

1. Why is it so important to *decide* to wait?

2. The statement is made that a person must decide and if his heart is basically right with God the wrong decision may be better then no decision. What do you think? Is this true if one is unwilling to take the responsibility and work to obtain the facts to make a proper decision?

3. Have you ever "sat on" a decision? Explain the results. Have you ever been convinced that a decision was wrong when you did this?

30
STEP TEN: THE STAMP OF APPROVAL: GOD'S PEACE

"He will keep in *perfect peace* all those who trust in him, whose thoughts turn often to the Lord! . . . O Lord, we love to do your will! Our hearts' desire is to glorify your name" (Isaiah 26:3, 8 LB author's italics). What a tremendous promise to the obedient Christian! To the one living in God's will—not merely peace; *perfect* peace. He not only promises this perfect peace but He also wants it to characterize our lives.

The Scriptures speak of His peace as an umpire or arbitrator in our hearts. Colossians 3:15 puts it this way: "And let the peace (soul harmony which comes) from Christ rule (act as an umpire continually) in your hearts—deciding and settling with finality all questions that arise in your minds" (AMPLIFIED). *When we are living in God's will the peace of God will rule as an umpire that we are, in fact, in God's will.* When we prayerfully contemplate a course of action or a new step in our Christian life—God's peace will permeate our lives if the decision is of Him. This is one of the major functions of the Holy Spirit—to give peace, a deep, internal confidence that we are in His will (*see* John 14–16).

One could compare it to a compass. The more our life points to God's perfect will the more His sanction of peace will rest upon us. There will be inward joy and reassurance that we are walking in the light.

Therefore, after you have taken the steps described in previous chapters you can be assured that if a pondered decision is in God's perfect will, there will be an increasing sense of rightness, oughtness, and peace. This sense may start as a gentle internal impression or feeling, but it will grow as time passes and you are continuing to feed on God's Word and pray. This is God's stamp of approval or umpire in your life.

This does not mean that the person living in God's will is free from problems or difficulties. In the same verse that He assures us of His inward peace, He reminds us that we will have "trials," "tribulation," and "sorrows" in the world (*see* John 16:33 RSV, LB). In fact, there may be brief periods of time when there is turmoil, anguish, or "agitation of spirit" as is recorded of Christ during the time of a difficult decision (*see* John 12:27; 13:21 LB, AMPLIFIED, NEB). Peter was "inwardly perplexed" when God was leading Him into a new area of service (*see* Acts 10:17). There may be a brief time of struggle with the flesh as our wills are aligned with His. During this time what is God's will is very clear through the major guideposts described earlier and a deep sense of oughtness from the Holy Spirit. As we yield our will to God's the oughtness will be accompanied by the growing peace of the Comforter (*see* Acts 9:31 LB). This peace will increase as we continue to *live God's will.*

"Now may the Lord of peace himself give you peace at all times in all ways" (2 Thessalonians 3:16).

QUESTIONS

1. If a person feels peace in his heart does this mean he is in God's will? (*See* Proverbs 16:2, 25.) If all is going well—does it mean the person is in God's will?

2. Do you really think Christ was perplexed, puzzled, had anguish of soul, or deep agitation? Did Christ have to align His will with the Father's?

3. Do you believe every decision needs positive subjective feelings?

PART FOUR

31
SUMMARY AND CHECKLIST

Christ once told His disciples, "I have still many things to say to you, but you are not able to bear them *nor* to take them upon you *nor* to grasp them now" (John 16:12 AMPLIFIED). In the preceding pages I have covered how to know and live God's will in a comprehensive way. If you are a young Christian some of the points covered are for you now—others as you mature and are confronted with the more difficult decisions required to do His will. However, you can be assured that at any stage in your Christian life His will is never more complicated or difficult than you are able to follow (*see* 1 John 5:3).

Regardless of your degree of maturity as a Christian, let me briefly reiterate the basics in our living God's will. The first step, obviously, is that you have accepted Jesus Christ as your personal Saviour through faith. The second step is to confess and appropriately deal with any known sin that the Holy Spirit reveals to you. The third step is to start feeding on God's Word, the Bible. If you are not familiar with it, I would suggest that you start reading in the New Testament. Read the Gospel of Mark or John and then read through the New Testament. Absorb what you can, and what you don't understand put aside for the time being. Try to read the Scriptures daily. Spend some time each day in prayer, asking God to direct you. Get to know some Christians who really want to know and please God and fellowship with them. As you do these simple things God will reveal more and more of His will to you. Later you may want to reconsider portions of this book as you continue in His will.

CHECKLIST TO CONSIDER BEFORE MAKING ANY MAJOR DECISION IN YOUR LIFE

Below is a summary of the steps for knowing God's will in a particular matter. They are arranged in the form of a checklist to help alert you to factors that might need to be dealt with before God will reveal His will to you. Use a pencil and answer the questions either in the book or on a separate sheet of paper.

The matter you want to know God's will in is:

_____

_____

Step 1: **Be obedient to His already revealed will**

A. Have you accepted Jesus Christ as your personal Saviour?   Yes___ No___

B. Is there any known sin in your life?   No___ Yes___

C. Are you being obedient to God's will to the extent to which it is now revealed?   Yes___ No___

Step 2: **Be open to any means or results**

A. Are you willing to follow God's will when He reveals it to you, regardless of what His will is or what it might cost you?   Yes___ No___

B. Are you open to any means He might choose to lead you, whether supernatural-miraculous or some less dramatic means?   Yes___ No___

Step 3: **God's Word: the cornerstone of guidance**

A. Do you have an adequate intake of God's Word?   Yes___ No___

B. Are you familiar with what the Scriptures really say about the issue for which you are seeking guidance?   Yes____ No____

Step 4: **Prayer**

A. Do you have a daily prayer time when you seek God's will and fellowship with Him?   Yes____ No____

B. Have you specifically asked God's will regarding the matter for which you are seeking His guidance?   Yes____ No____

C. Are you too busy to adequately meditate and wait on Him?   No____ Yes____

Step 5: **The Holy Spirit**

A. Have you acknowledged the presence and function of the Holy Spirit in your life?   Yes____ No____

B. Does the Holy Spirit now fill your life?   Yes____ No____

Step 6: **Counsel**

A. Do you consistently fellowship with other Christians and hear God's Word proclaimed?   Yes____ No____

B. Is there any possibility of a medical problem for which you should obtain help?   No____ Yes____

C. Should you specifically seek the counsel of another, whether a minister, Christian friend, professional counselor, etc.?   No____ Yes____

Step 7: **Providential circumstances**

A. Have you adequately considered the Providential circumstances that are available to you?   Yes____ No____

Step 8: **Evaluation**

A. Are you tired?   No____ Yes____

B. Have you specifically evaluated the reasons for and against the decision you are considering and your underlying motives (preferably on paper)? Yes____ No____

C. Have you considered the needs of the world around you? Yes____ No____

D. Have you considered your own abilities? Yes____ No____

E. Have you considered your own desires and whether or not they are possible within God's will? Yes____ No____

F. Will your decision harm your body or hurt others? No____ Yes____

G. Will it hinder your spiritual growth, walk with Christ, or testimony? No____ Yes____

H. Will it hinder the spiritual growth of others? No____ Yes____

I. Is it the choice that is most pleasing to God? Yes____ No____

J. Is it the best and wisest choice using your enlightened judgment? Yes____ No____

K. Have you prayerfully evaluated the matter alone, without unnecessary time pressure? Yes____ No____

Prayerfully consider all of the above points—especially any responses in the right-hand column. These responses may indicate some action you need to take before you will be able to come to a conclusion about God's will in the matter.

List any steps that should be done before you conclude

what God's will is in the matter. _____

_____

_____

Is there anything else He wants you to do or consider?

_____

_____

Step 9: **The decision: to wait or to act**

Should you postpone the decision as to what God's will is in the matter?_____

Should you decide but wait for its fulfillment? _____

You already know God's will but not His timing; therefore, must you patiently wait His time? _____

Or should you now come to a deliberate decision on what His will is? If so, what is that decision?_____

_____

Step 10: **The stamp of approval: God's peace**

Having determined God's will in the matter, do you have a deep, inward peace about the decision? As time passes and you continue to reflect and pray about the decision, do you have an increasing assurance from Him that the decision was the right one? If so, proceed accordingly.

Epilogue

I firmly believe God's will is knowable—but the reason we often are confused about His will is that we don't meet the prerequisites or else we barge ahead, unwilling to wait for His leading in our corporate or individual lives.

However, I want to make several points very clear. First, though I may write on the subject and believe I have some insights—I am a pilgrim—learning, growing, and sometimes struggling in my walk with Him. By the time this book is published I may have some new insights on God's will and wish I could modify others expressed on these pages. The point is that none of us has ever "arrived" so long as we have our mortal bodies. This is especially true in so crucial and all-inclusive a subject as knowing God's will for our lives.

The second point is that our walk is by faith. Step-by-step answers and checklists are nothing more than helps—they can make a definite contribution—but they will never eliminate our need to walk by faith, keeping our eyes on Christ. Also, since our walk is dynamic there are always some new opportunities and decisions that must be made regarding His will. This keeps us humble, dependent, and seeking Him and His will in some new area at all times. May God bless you and me as we endeavor to follow our wonderful Lord and Saviour, Jesus Christ.

"May He give us the desire to do his will in everything . . ." (1 Kings 8:58 LB).